The Spoken Blessing

A Spiritual Posture

Ann Dews Gleaton

TATE PUBLISHING, LLC

ISBN: 1-9331489-6-9

Dedication

To every individual, couple, family and group of believers
who long to have the Spoken Blessing operate *within*
and *through* their lives. . . . to the glory of God
and for the furtherance of His Kingdom.

Acknowledgements

I am forever grateful to my Savior and Lord, Jesus. You have drawn me to You with love and tenderness, firmness and instruction. Thank you for never leaving nor forsaking me. Thank you for walking and talking with me every day, sharing with me Your precious intimacies and powerful revelations. You are everything to me.

To the man of my dreams, my knight in shining armor: my wonderful husband, Cal; I love you. You are my best friend, the one who touches my heart and soothes my soul. Thank you for walking with me through these years of learning, studying, and teaching; failing and succeeding. Thank you for being there with me.

Our four incredible children: Anthony, Peyton, Elizabeth and David are my joy and inspiration for imparting God's blessings. You have brought me so much pleasure in life that I just have to brag and show everyone your pictures. You have made this momma proud! You truly are God's gifts to me!

Charlie and Blanche Dews, my sweet parents, sowed the good seeds of faith, hope and trust. Mom, thank you for all the hours of caring for David, cooking our meals and baking sweet treats. . . . your labors of love. Dad, thank you for setting the example of optimism, and a happy heart. I am deeply grateful that the Lord brought both of you to Tallahassee!

To my sisters, Marti Sappenfield and Libby Markham and husband, Gary: you have played an important part in my learning how to give and receive God's blessings. Your faithful interest and love have encouraged me to pursue success. Thank you for your loving support.

Jeanette Gleaton, my mother-in-law, has taught me the sweetness of Jesus. Your servant's heart has challenged my personal walk and motivated me to a more humble, Christ-like servitude. You have been an inspiration to me.

To Jo Anne Arnett and Laura Mann of the Center for Biblical Studies in Tallahassee and Dena Woodburn: you have been loyal friends, supporting and encouraging me as I pressed on toward the vision God has given. Thank you for providing me opportunities to refine this message and to develop this principle into a ministry that is impacting many lives. You are very special to me.

To Robert A. Shelley, Kathy Palmer and Dr. Bill Lyons of Tallahassee, Florida, David and Carol Peleggi of Jerusalem, Israel and Pastor Bill Ligon, of Brunswick, Georgia: you have my deepest appreciation for helping me understand and value our rich, Christian heritage as it has been carried forth by the Jewish people—their culture, their language and their faith in the one, true God.

To Pastor Eli Hendricks and Kelly: you have exemplified lives filled with confidence and hope in Jesus. You have loved and trained our children with great patience, always affirming and supporting them. Thank you for your leadership and faithful friendship.

To my pastor, Dr. Richard N. Ledford, II: your zeal and passion for sharing the gospel of Jesus Christ has intensified the fire that was burning within me. Thank you for carrying the baton of God's vision for the Body of Christ. You, Andrea and the boys are very dear to my family.

My love and appreciation go to my friends at Christian Heritage Church in Tallahassee, Florida, who listened and learned, tried and tested *The Spoken Blessing,* discovering it to be God's treasure hidden in the depths of His Word. I am thrilled that you have become "the church who blesses."

Ann Dews Gleaton

A Special Note of Thanks

To Dr. Richard Tate: Cal and I were excited by your enthusiasm and sincere interest in the concept of this book. Our confidence was boosted as we watched you embrace the vision God has given. The fire in your heart ignited the glowing embers in ours. We needed your support!

I am deeply grateful for my editor, Rita Tate, and the staff of Tate Publishing. Your commitment to completing this message has blessed me and honored God. Thank you for allowing God's Spirit to direct your talents and creativity to refine this book. You have proven yourself to be faithful to God and to His vision.

What encouragement and motivation my friends, Randy, Karla and Brody Enwright of Tallahassee, Florida, have given me over the years. You have been instrumental in sharing God's message through the giving of thousands of blessings. Through your walk in life, you have imparted blessings to the President, to congressmen and women, judges and attorney generals, to taxi cab drivers, waiters and waitresses, to children, teachers, neighbors and friends, to pastors and prisoners, just to name a few. I anticipate a great, eternal reward for your perseverance and love. Thank you for being my co-laborers.

To Cassidy Webb and Kyle DelVecchio who have multiplied our joy of having and raising children: you have added your love, laughter, friendship and support to our family. I am proud of you and am excited about God's wonderful provision for your lives.

With a humble heart, I say: "thank you, thank you, thank you" to my prayer team. You were faithful to pray for me as I wrote and wrote. Every week you inquired about the book. Every day you prayed. I needed you and you were there for me. Thank you my dear family and friends.

I love you.

~ **Ann**

Table of Contents

Foreword

In August of 2001, my life took a drastic change that my family and I thought would be the most difficult undertaking of our 15 years of ministry. After much prayer we accepted the call of God to pastor an almost 100-year-old Pentecostal Holiness Church in Tallahassee, Florida. Having pioneered two churches in different parts of the country, we were unsure what lay ahead of us in taking an established congregation that we felt had the potential to become a great regional presence for the glory of the Lord. As any new pastor will do, we set about getting to know the families and leaders of this new body we now led. I will never forget the day that Ann Gleaton and her husband, Cal, were introduced into our lives. Through Ann, and her gift of encouragement, our work here has been the easiest assignment God has given us.

Meeting Ann Gleaton is much like walking out of a dark room into a beautiful day of bright sunshine. The glory of God on her countenance is always a fresh respite from the burdens and cares that ministry can sometimes bring. I will always cherish our first meeting in which Ann boldly proclaimed, "Pastor Ledford, I just want to speak a blessing over you and your ministry to our church and city." As I bowed my head, I felt the sweet presence of the Lord flood through my soul and I was greatly encouraged as Ann began not to pray, but boldly declare the blessings of God over all that lay ahead of us. I will forever be indebted to Ann for all I have learned as a leader, pastor, husband, and father from her teaching on *The Spoken Blessing*.

This book is not about some hypothetical revelation, this book is a practical tool proven by the life work of Ann Gleaton. I can attest to the fact that her family and countless others have benefited from embracing this biblical truth of speaking the blessing of God. My life and ministry have been wonderfully energized by these time-tested nuggets of God that Ann reveals in this book. I encourage you to allow this book to flood your spirit and put to practice the revelation held within. You, your family, and ministry will never be the same again after learning how to appropriate *The Spoken Blessing*.

Dr. Richard N. Ledford II
Sr. Pastor, Christian Heritage Church
Tallahassee, Florida

Preface

Sharing Shadows

Muffled weeping came from his room. The figure in the bed was undisturbed by the sounds. His sleep was deep even though his room was full of sorrow. Across the bed, the street light cast a shadow of the towering water oak which loomed outside. The weeping came from one who shared her shadow with the oak. The sadness in this mother's heart was as dark as those blended shadows. Another shouting match, harsh, condemning words and an order to, "Go to your room and just go to bed!" had ended this long day.

Thoughts of her son's life; his past, his present and the predictable future ran through this mother's mind like a movie. In kindergarten, he had been labeled a "trouble-maker" and on numerous occasions, had been sent to stand, facing the corner. Upon completion of that year, his attitude was summed up with one statement: "I hate school!" By the time third grade rolled around, his teacher came to the conclusion that this dear student was an ADHD, {Attention Deficit/Hyperactivity Disorder} child. She wanted him tested and placed on medication to help him pay more attention to his work. This student became angrier by the day. He hated himself because he appeared different from other students. He hated his parents for subjecting him to humiliating psychological testing. He despised walking in the shadow of his older brother and being pestered by his younger sister. Basically, he hated everyone, including God. Walls of resentment and frustration were blocking this child from feeling, feeling anything, but anger. Acts of kindness could not penetrate those walls. And that's why his mother was weeping. Hardened hearts and towering walls pointed toward a predictable future: jail time. His mother had lived long enough to have witnessed the relationship of angry hearts, embittered minds and self-destruction. "No, God, no. Not my son. Don't let it happen to him. I love him so. I hate the way things are. I don't want him to grow up like me."

Her weeping continued, but it was no longer on behalf of her son. She wept over her past; her hardened heart, her bitterness, her unwillingness to forgive. She knew first-hand how destructive those walls around a heart could be to relationships and to one's future. Years, and years, and many years had been allowed to pass without reconciliation. "Oh, God, things have to change. Help us, God. Help me."

This humbled shadow separated from that of the towering oak as it quietly moved into the darkened house. Weary from crying and weary from worrying, the mother slipped back into her bed. Sleep came, but with a struggle. Life was a struggle, but others weren't to know. She had learned to "grin and bear it," "stuff it and shove it on down." It was no wonder that she suffered from digestive problems. This mother was definitely feeling the effects of the unresolved emotional upheaval that her family was experiencing. Yes, it was affecting the entire family.

A major overhaul, that's what was needed.

The Man with a Message

Not long after her night of weeping, this mother heard about a guest speaker who was coming to their church. Pastor Bill Ligon was the son-in-law of some church members. His presentation concentrated on *Imparting the Blessing*. How that related to her, she wasn't sure, but she insisted that she and her husband attend.

At the conclusion of Pastor Ligon's teaching, this mother felt the gratitude and relief of one who had been thrown a life-ring as they struggled in a stormy sea. As one being lifted from the overpowering waves, her thoughts screamed through her mind: "Life, not death, is my future. Hope, not despair, can fill my life. Joy, and not sorrow, will overflow from my heart." Things began to change for this mother, for this son, for the whole family as they began to use the principle of the *Blessing*. Blessings were given and blessings were received, most of the time. Those old walls didn't fall down overnight. Rome wasn't built in a day. But those parents did not give up. God had told them to love, love and keep on loving that son, even when he didn't love back. Hug, hug and keep on hugging. Bless him in his going out and bless him in his coming in. These parents had to commit to change; change their attitudes, their focus, their hearts.

Dear friends, the family crisis I just described is a "true story." It is *our* story. The people, the places, the hurts, the painful words and attitudes are real. And so is our God. He was, is and shall be our Life, our Redeemer and Restorer. He can be yours, as well. The message: the principle of the *Spoken Blessing* is His message, His 'sent' word for you and yours at this time. The timing is now. Take this message and use it within your family, your friends, your work associates, your fellow believers, and, yes, even, strangers. Offer them a cup of cool, refreshing, life-changing water. They will be forever grateful to you and to our God. I know, because *I* am . . . forever grateful.

~ *Ann Dews Gleaton*

Introduction

The Spoken Blessing

A Spiritual Posture

Many individuals are familiar with 'saying the blessing' before eating their meal. A word of thanks to God is often spoken aloud within the group that is eating or simply thought within one's heart and mind.

That type of blessing is *not* the focus of this book.

Some people ask God to bless others and themselves, as Jabez did in I Chronicles 4:10——

> *"Oh that Thou wouldst bless me indeed,*
> *and enlarge my border,*
> *and that Thy hand might be with me,*
> *and that Thou wouldst keep me from harm,*
> *and that it may not pain me!"*

This type of request is often associated with a petition to God, either spoken aloud or silently.

That type of blessing is **not** the foundation of this book.

The focus and foundation of this book is the *Spoken Blessing,* a term I use to describe a rule of conduct I observed occurring within the Bible. From the release of God's creative words which formed His new world, through the verbalized faith of the ancient patriarchs as they trusted God to dwell in the midst of their loved ones, to the impartation of Jesus as he blessed the young children, I recognized a powerful consequence in the *spoken* release of the word of God. God's *original desire* was for His image to be multiplied across the face of His world:

"Let Us make man in Our image, according to Our likeness . . ." (Genesis 1:26). Verbalized faith is essential to fulfilling God's *original instruction* to His creations: "Be fruitful and multiply, and fill the earth . . ." (Genesis 1:28). God gave mankind the ability to communicate with Him and with others. Faith in God can be multiplied within others as we speak of His mercy and grace. We can verbalize our experience and expectation of His goodness, helping others to recognize and value Him. Valuing God is vital to one's embracing Him. As we speak of His nature, we speak of His image, that is: who He is and what He does. Communicating this to others is a way of increasing His image across the world.

May the Lord counsel your mind as you
carefully read and digest this book.
May the eyes of your heart be enlighened
so that you may know
what is the hope of His calling, what are
the riches of the glory of His
inheritance in the saints,
and what is the surpassing greatness
of His power toward you who believe.
Ephesians 1:18,19

"A wise man will be satisfied with good by the fruit of
his words, and the deeds of a man's hands will return to him.
The way of a fool is right in his own eyes,
But a wise man is he who listens to counsel."
Proverbs 12:14–15

Beloved reader, what *posture* do you assume before the Lord and before others? Do you listen to "counsel" or, are you and your perspective always right? How teachable are you? Will you allow others to correct you? Are you being satisfied "with good?" Can you discern the type of seeds you have sown? What type of harvest are you reaping? Do you need understanding for things that are happening within your life?

" . . . those who seek the LORD understand all things."
Proverbs 28:5

As you seek the Lord, He will help you distinguish between good and evil. He will provide you insight into the situations and events that occur in your life.

"But if any of you lacks wisdom, let him ask of God, who gives to all men generously and without reproach, and it will be given to him."
James 1:5

Asking for help requires humility.

Several years ago, I used a hairdresser who was an immigrant. She had "made it on her own." This lady was very proud of her accomplishments and success. God placed us together for a reason. As the months passed, I talked with her about my relationship with the Lord. One day, I inquired if she had ever asked Jesus to be her personal Savior. She quickly snapped back: "No! I've never asked anybody for anything!" We read in Mark 6:1–6 that even Jesus could do only a few miracles within the people of his hometown due to their unbelief. We should assume a posture of humility to ASK God for something, to listen to and respond to His reply. We should strive to become a *true disciple* of Christ, following Him, learning His ways.

If we are a New Testament, New Covenant disciple, then we are not a mere pupil or learner. We adhere to and accept the Lord's instruction that He gives us. We make His instruction our rule of conduct. We become so familiar with the Lord's character and workings that we recognize His hand throughout the Word and within our lives. To know the Lord, we must spend time with Him. The Lord created us for the pleasure of knowing us, so let's walk and talk with Him, learning His heart's desire, discovering what brings Him joy and excitement. Let us humble ourselves and our desires, to support and assume His goals as *our* lifetime ambitions.

Consider the disciples who walked and talked with Jesus along the well-known Emmaus Road. Why didn't they *recognize* Jesus?

> *"But their eyes were prevented from recognizing Him."*
> **Luke 24:16**

What *prevented* these disciples from recognizing Jesus?

> *"And He said to them, 'O foolish men*
> *and slow of heart to believe in*
> *all that the prophets have spoken!'"*
> **Luke 24:25**

Jesus described these disciples as unable to comprehend the precepts and principles of God's Kingdom. He identified the disciples as being slow to embrace and apply His Kingship to the spiritual realm. He understood that they were focusing on their immediate and pressing need for relief from the oppression of Roman rule and dictatorship. Their interpretation and expectation of Jesus' purpose "was right in their own eyes." They had a need and they expected Him to meet that need according to *their* way of thinking. They had not humbled themselves to God's purpose for His Messiah. They had been focusing more on their "woes" than on God's "wows."

They had been focusing more on their "woes" than on God's "wows."

The disciples' perception of Jesus affected their ability to recognize or to become well acquainted with Him. Jesus effectively used this situation to God's glory, counseling His disciples and correcting their way of thinking.

The effect that Jesus' Emmaus Road teaching had on those disciples was quite remarkable. Consider their demeanor as Jesus joined them as they walked toward Emmaus.

"And they stood still, looking sad and downcast."
Luke 24:17 AMP

Their "spiritual posture" changed that night.

Once Jesus had explained the Scriptures to them, once their eyes had been opened to recognize Jesus and their hearts were stirred to believe, their words and actions became excited and uplifted. The disciples were no longer slow or sluggish. They couldn't contain their joy. Their "spiritual posture" changed that night. That very night, they retraced their steps those seven miles and returned to Jerusalem. Their "woes" had been changed to "wows." They had to tell the others. They wanted their new faith in Jesus, their understanding of the Scriptures, to be shared and multiplied within their friends.

And so it is with me. As I share the principle of the *Spoken Blessing,* may your "woes" be changed to "wows." May the insights into the Scriptures bring new life, energy and excitement into the very core of your faith in Jesus.

Chapter 1

Who Began Using the Spoken Blessing?

"And God created the great sea monsters,
and every living creature that moves,
with which the waters swarmed after their kind,
and every winged bird after its kind;
and God saw that it was good.
And God blessed them, saying, 'Be fruitful and multiply,
and fill the waters in the seas, and let
birds multiply on the earth.' "
Genesis 1:21–22

In the beginning, God used the Spoken Blessing to *impart the ability to fulfill His plan.* God knew the power of His words; the creative force behind them. He desired for His creation, for the Animal Kingdom, to increase in numbers, extending their existence across His newly-formed earth. Make a "side note" of this thought (A side note is a special notation to be written to the side of your page, highlighting that thought or suggestion for future consideration.): *If God blessed His animals for multiplication, can we not bless and call forth increase over our animals or those things that are in our care?*

"Then God said, 'Let Us make man in Our image,
according to Our likeness;
and let them rule over the fish of the sea and
over the birds of the sky and

over the cattle and over all the earth,
and over every creeping thing that creeps on the earth.'
And God created man in His own image,
in the image of God He created him;
male and female He created them.
And God blessed them; and God said to them,
'Be fruitful and multiply, and fill the earth, and subdue it;
and rule over the fish of the sea and
over the birds of the sky,
and over every living thing that moves on the earth.'"
Genesis 1:26–28

God's plan was for His image and likeness to be multiplied across the face of the earth. He desired for His character to permeate His created world. Adam and Eve were to serve as His representatives across the earth, having been formed in His image. They had a body, soul and spirit made in the pattern or likeness of the Holy Trinity.

He blessed them with the ability to fulfill His plan.

God assigned Adam and Eve dominion over His creation. This first couple was given authority and responsibility to cultivate and keep the Garden of Eden. He blessed them with the ability to fulfill His plan.

The service of cultivating or working can be directed toward things, people or God. Likewise, Adam and Eve were to keep, care for, guard and preserve the Garden. This is a beautiful and accurate picture of what the *Spoken Blessing* can do within a person's life. It prepares, breaks up, prevents, preserves, improves, refines, develops and promotes God's perfect and divine plan for every person.

From the beginning, God has desired for His creation to

be blessed and to bless. His instruction was for "blessings" and "increase" to fill, replenish and cultivate His creation. God knew that sin would challenge the fulfillment of His plan. He knew that Adam and Eve would be forced out of their Paradise and into a harsher world of toil and trouble. God knew that their confidence might suffer defeat. But, He had blessed them. And this couple remembered His blessing and impartation of the ability to "be fruitful and multiply."

"Now the man had relations with his wife Eve,
and she conceived and gave birth to Cain, and she said,
'I have gotten a manchild with the help of the LORD.'"
Genesis 4:1

Eve recognized the faithfulness of God and His power to fulfill His Spoken Word. Surely, her confidence increased as she gave birth to her sons, Cain and Able. Even after the death of Able, Eve affirmed her faith in God as she gave birth to another son, Seth:

"God has appointed me another offspring
in place of Able; for Cain killed him."
Genesis 4:25

Eve focused her faith and honor toward God, the One who had dominion and power over her life and the future of her family. Her offspring continued to "be fruitful and multiply" as Seth had a son, Enosh. Her influence of faith is chronicled:

"Then men began to call upon the name of the LORD."
Genesis 4:26

Men wanted the help of God in their lives. They understood that He was their source. The Scriptures gave prominence to another man who recognized that God was His source.

"These are the records of the generations of Noah.
Noah was a righteous man, blameless in his time;
Noah walked with God."
Genesis 6:9

Building upon the strength of Noah's relationship with Him, God commanded Noah to construct an ark. God's faithfulness sustained Noah during his prolonged effort amidst a community of evil and berating people.

"By faith Noah, being warned by God
about things not yet seen,
in reverence, prepared an ark for the
salvation of his household,
by which he condemned the world,
and became an heir of the righteousness
which is according to faith."
Hebrews 11:7

Noah was a part of God's plan. The ark was a beautiful foreshadowing of the secret hiding place: the place of refuge that Jesus offers you and me. The ark of Noah saved mankind from total destruction. Jesus saved mankind from total *eternal* destruction. He is our shelter from the storm. He carries us through troubled waters. He offers us protection from the elements of sin and offers provision for us: body, soul and spirit.

Now, catch this: " . . . Noah, being warned by God about things not yet seen, . . ." describes our present day situation. The Word of God has warned us about events that we have not yet seen, nor can scarcely imagine. Yet, in reverence to our Almighty, All-knowing God, we must help build the ark of Jesus within our family, friends, and others.

As he chopped and chiseled, lifted and loaded, Noah spoke of God.

I suspect that Noah evangelized those who came around during the many years he spent building. The Bible documents that Noah had brothers and sisters (Genesis 5:30). Don't you think that Noah would have tried to share his faith in God with his family members, as well as others in his community? As he chopped and chiseled, lifted and loaded, Noah spoke of God.

"So then faith cometh by hearing, and
hearing by the word of God."
Romans 10:17 KJV

Remember, Noah walked with God, therefore, Noah HEARD the words of God. As he repeated what God had said, Noah's faith was reinforced and his confidence strengthened. In spite of the taunting and mocking, Noah was able to complete God's command.

As we speak a blessing, which is based on the powerful word of God, we exemplify our faith in Him, placing our focus and trust on His steadfast character.

Imagine that you are walking through a large shopping mall and notice someone looking up. You also notice that their focus is fixed. You wonder: "What in the world could be so intriguing?" So, you look up. Then, you see it and gasp at its beauty. Your arm, hand and finger work instinctively, together, pointing upward. Excitedly, you exclaim, "There it is, I see it. It is beautiful!" Others gather around. The excitement and focus works like a magnet drawing many to peer upward.

That's exactly what will happen when you begin to use the *Spoken Blessing*. How can I be so sure? My husband, Cal, and I have been speaking blessings over our children for more than thirteen years. The Preface related how our family had hit 'rock bottom.' The only way to look was 'up.' We gradually learned how to redirect our focus on God's Word and what He declared about our children, our situations, and our future.

God established the example of blessing children as He blessed Noah and his SONS, after Noah had prepared an altar and offered burnt offerings to God (Genesis 8:20–9:1–3). We know that God blessed His creation from the beginning and that He wanted the original *impartation of the ability to fulfill His plan* to be continued. Also, take note that within His blessing was His *provision*. Review Genesis 9:1–3, 7–17 and discover how unceasing God intended His blessings to be.

Blessings have a long-term effect.

Let's look ahead several generations past Noah, and read about one of his descendants, Abram. The continuous, long-term effect of God's blessings becomes evident as we read His communication with Abram:

> *"Now the LORD said to Abram,*
> *'Go forth from your country, and from your relatives*
> *and from your father's house, to the land which I will show you;*
> *and I will make you a great nation, and I will bless you,*
> *and make your name great; and so you shall be a blessing;*
> *and I will bless those who bless you,*
> *and the one who curses you I will curse.*
> *And in you all the families of the earth shall be blessed.'"*
> ***Genesis 12:1–3***

God fully intended for His blessing to *flow into* and *through* people.

The Hebrew word used for "bless" is BARAK which means: to kneel down, to bless; praise, to be blessed, pray to, to invoke, to ask a blessing; to greet; to curse; the rendering 'curse' is a Hebrew euphemism.

"Blessing" is the English translation of BRAKAH which means a blessing, benediction, benefit, favor, peace, invocation of good; a happy, or blessed man.

In studying God's Word, I often use Webster's Dictionary to help me understand a word used to define some other word; i.e.: "invoke" means "to call on God for a blessing, help; inspiration, protection; to ask solemnly for; implore; entreat."

In these verses, the word "make" is translated from the Hebrew word ASAH: to work, to labor, to create, to construct, to build, to accomplish, to prepare, to keep; to fulfill, to be made; to sacrifice; to appoint. This word describes God's creative activity; the fashioning and refining of His work.

If God is going to "make" Abram's name "great," He will be very active in this work. God will be laboring, creating, building, refining and fashioning Abram into the man, the husband, the father, the patriarch of a mighty group of people.

When we consider God's original blessing over Adam and Eve, we recall that He intended for there to be 'labor' and 'cultivation' of that blessing within their lives. In the same way, God committed Himself to such 'labor' on behalf of Abram, Sarai and their future family.

Will God do any less for us? We are the future families of which God spoke in His blessing Abram:

"And in you all the families of the earth shall be blessed."
Genesis 12:3

"Is God the God of Jews only?
Is He not the God of Gentiles also?
Yes, of Gentiles also,
Since indeed God who will justify the circumcised by faith

And the uncircumcised through faith is one."
Romans 3:29–30

"For you are all sons of God through faith in Christ Jesus.
For all of you who were baptized into Christ
have clothed yourselves with Christ.
There is neither Jew nor Greek, there is
neither slave nor free man, there is
neither male nor female; for you are all one in Christ Jesus.
And if you belong to Christ, then you are Abraham's offspring,
heirs according to promise."
Galatians 3:26–29

God is God to the Jews and the Gentiles. God desires for us to be successful and prosper within His Kingdom, therefore, we can feel confident that He desires to bless us, to labor and work within our lives just as He desired to and executed His plans in the lives of Abram and Sarai.

"for it is God who is at work in you, both to will
and to work for His good pleasure."
Philippians 2:13

Some may question if God *favors* the Jewish people more than the Gentiles. Carefully consider the story in Acts 10. Read this account of Cornelius and the consequences of his reverence toward God, his diligence to seek God through prayer, and his continual effort to honor the Jewish people. Discover the truth that Peter did:

" . . . I most certainly understand now that God
is not one to show partiality, but in every
nation the man who fears Him and does
what is right, is welcome to Him."
Acts 10:34–35

In the Middle Eastern culture, males were, and still are, more valued and esteemed than females. Therefore, I found it interesting to discover that Moses, in the writing of Genesis, made a special note of the blessing spoken over Rebekah, a female. Keep in mind that God's original plan and blessing transcended all cultural boundaries which may have restricted a subgroup of people. Turn to Genesis 24 and read Rebekah's blessing. Pay close attention to verse 60:

"And they blessed Rebekah and said to her,
'May you, our sister, become thousands of ten thousands,
and may your descendants possess the
gate of those who hate them.'"

The phrase 'thousands of ten thousands' is used figuratively to represent the extreme; an indefinite number or one that is innumerable. Rebekah's family expected great increase, dominion and authority to flow into and through her life. They lived a life in submission and recognition of the Lord's authority over them.

"And he (Laban) said, 'Come in, blessed of the LORD!'"
Genesis 24:31

"Then Laban and Bethuel answered and said,
'The matter comes from the LORD; so we cannot speak to
you bad or good. Behold, Rebekah is
before you, take her and go,
and let her be the wife of your master's
son, as the LORD has spoken.'"
Genesis 24:50–51

Consider this: Rebekah did become the mother of thousands, truly, millions. By the time Moses led the children of

Israel out of Egypt, their numbers had grown to millions. Review God's blessing that He spoke over Abram in Genesis 12:1–3.

> *"And I will make you a great nation, and I bless you,*
> *and make your name great;"*
> **Genesis 12:2**

Through God's perfect design and plan, He coupled these two blessings to complement each other.

Abram's son, Isaac, carried that blessing into his marriage with Rebekah. Through God's perfect design and plan, He coupled these two blessings to complement each other. Webster's helps us here: "complement;" is "that which completes or brings to perfection."

Let's make a Life Application at this point.

Life Application:

Cal and I have spoken blessings over our children since their youth. Within those blessings, we have released, by faith, God's provision for their spouses and children. We are confident that God will direct our children to the one He has prepared for them, just as He directed Abraham's servant across hundreds of miles to locate Abraham's relatives. Across the distance of time, God will bring forth spouses who carry a blessing complementing, *bringing into perfection,* those blessings we have spoken over our children. This statement may arouse indignation within some readers. However, bear with me. I recognize that a person can remain single for their entire life and feel *completed* through their relationship with the Lord (Matthew 19:10–12). I do not deny that. Yet, Cal and I can personally testify to God's complementing our individual gifting and calling through each other. I may not be adept or proficient in something, but Cal is. . . . and vice versa. We appreciate each other's abilities and assist the other when needed. Unity, oneness in body, soul and spirit, is our goal, as is God's goal. He has declared us as 'one,' therefore we equally share in the honor of serving Him and share in the responsibility and authority of serving others. We are co-laborers in God's Kingdom. *"And the two shall become one . . ."* (Matthew 19:5–6; Genesis 2:24).

Remember: the Spoken Blessing is used to *impart the ability to fulfill God's plan.* We must, continually, direct our faith, focus and speech to God's ultimate, eternal purposes.

> *" . . . Thy Kingdom come, Thy will be done, on earth as it is in heaven."*
> ***Matthew 6:10***

Within the well-known Lord's Prayer, Jesus was instructing His disciples on the importance of their submission to God's ultimate plans and purposes for His kingdom. We can learn from this example; i.e.: keep our eyes on our eternal destiny and the furtherance of God's Kingdom.

Return with me to the continued saga of Isaac and Rebekah. Read Genesis 26:1–5. Look at God's blessing that was spoken over Isaac. Does it not repeat and confirm His blessing for Abraham?

> *"Now Isaac sowed in that land, and reaped in the same year a hundredfold. And the LORD blessed him, and the man became rich, and continued to grow richer until he became very wealthy; for he had possessions of flocks and herds and a great household,*

so that the Philistines envied him."
Genesis 26:12–14

After Isaac experienced repeated conflict with his 'neighbors,' he found a place of rest and called the well "Rehoboth" which meant "plenty of room." He confessed his faith in God's provision and commitment to His blessing as noted in Genesis 26:22:

"At last the LORD has made room for us,
and we shall be fruitful in the land."

Take note that it was *after* Isaac's confession with his mouth which reflected the conviction of his heart, that God appeared to him, reassuring Isaac of His eternal destiny for him:

"I am the God of your father Abraham;
do not fear, for I am with you.
I will bless you, and multiply your descendants,
for the sake of My servant Abraham."
Genesis 26:24

Isaac had personally experienced the spoken blessing of God and the fulfillment of His word. God set forth the example of speaking blessings over others, therefore it should not surprise us to observe Isaac's deep desire to bless his son, Esau, his firstborn. Turn to Genesis 27:1–4.

" . . . that my soul may bless you before I die."
Genesis 27:4

The Hebrew understanding of *soul* was the "inner self". Thus, Isaac indicated his deepest desire was to bless his son with everything that was within him. Isaac carried within his total inner being the blessing that God commanded over his father, Abraham, as well as, himself.

The Source of our blessing is God.

Much has been written about Rebekah and Jacob's deceiving Isaac that resulted in the younger brother, Jacob, receiving Esau's firstborn blessing. Throughout generations, the Bible documented that great value was placed on the blessing of the firstborn son, for it confirmed his birthright which carried pre-eminence, authority and provision. God had spoken to Rebekah when she was still carrying her twins. He explained His plans for her boys:

" . . . Two nations are in your womb; and
two peoples shall be separated
from your body; and one people shall
be stronger than the other;
and the older shall serve the younger."
Genesis 25:23

. . . she stepped in to "help God out."

Before her boys were born, Rebekah knew that the younger, Jacob, would ultimately rule over his older brother, Esau. So, when she overheard Isaac instructing Esau to prepare a meal for his blessing, she *stepped in* to "help God out." She didn't trust God to accomplish what He said He would do. My, my, my, is that not a lesson for us! Just WHERE is our trust level? Is there anything too hard for the Lord (Genesis 18:14)? Our words will quickly say, "No!" Yet, what do our actions say?

Friends, be careful not to take matters into your own hands. Deception and defiance are insidious.

The blessings Cal and I have spoken over our children are based on God's Word, the life-giving Word of God. Our four children may not be experiencing *all* that we, by faith, have spoken over them, but, we cannot force those things to happen. If we try to shove these spiritual truths down their throats, they may regurgitate them. Our 'force feeding' them might cause our children spiritual nausea and repulsion, thus causing them to run from us and God. Balance comes from trusting God with the outcome and final authority over our children. This balance and our trust continue to develop. Has our trust been tested—stretched to its current limits? Has our balance been shaken? You bet it has. Our children have made mistakes, and unwise choices. So have we. AND, we have discovered the consequences for those choices. The Bible is full of examples of both; children and parents suffering the results of their actions. Rebekah truly suffered for her deception and rebellion. It cost her the pleasure of her favorite son's companionship. Rebekah continued her deception as she persuaded Isaac to send Jacob away:

> *"I am tired of living, because of the daughters of Heth;*
> *if Jacob takes a wife from the daughters of Heth,*
> *like these, from the daughters of the land,*
> *what good will my life be to me?"*
> **Genesis 27:46**

A question that every believer must answer is: "Do I trust God with the future?"

Picture this: you are in a thick crowd of people who are gradually shifting closer to the edge of the street. The police are controlling your advance, holding everyone at the curb. As the crowd, filled with anticipation, pushes closer together to see the approaching excitement, you notice a tall man hoisting a young child up to his shoulders. This pair looks expectantly as the man points in the direction of the advancing parade.

Let's apply this scenario to that of a parent who speaks blessings over their children. Every parent should deeply desire that their children succeed and prosper to a higher level or degree than they have. As devoted parents, we should "lift" our children onto our shoulders, helping them "see" and experience their future destiny that is "down the road" and soon to arrive. Releasing blessings into their lives can assist them in that effort.

Those who are blessing others are simply agreeing with God's original desire and plan for "fruitfulness" and "multiplication."

The Spoken Blessing places an expectation upon Almighty God to exercise His power, authority and blessing over people. Those who are blessing others are simply agreeing with God's original desire and plan for "fruitfulness" and "multiplication."

Why was Rebekah so forlorn? Could it be that she recognized her failure to assist her boys in attaining their God-appointed destiny. Painfully, she could have realized that she had worked AGAINST that fulfillment, attempting to 'help God out.'

Friends, please take this lesson to heart. Learn from it. Now, is anything too hard for the Lord? Absolutely not! His mercies are new every morning. His grace is sufficient for us! Thank you, Lord, thank you.

Did or will God ignore His covenant relationship with His people? Absolutely not! God responded to Isaac's blessing that he spoke over Jacob (Genesis 27:27–29). As Jacob lived out his life under that blessing, he followed his father's example by prophesying over and blessing his sons.

> *"Then Jacob summoned his sons and said,*
> *'Assemble yourselves that I may tell you what shall*
> *befall you in the days to come.'"*
> **Genesis 49:1**

Look at the definition of the word: *tell*. The Hebrew word is: *Nagad* which can mean—to bring to light, to declare, to announce; to celebrate with praise; to make known; to reveal something which one would not otherwise know.

As you read Jacob's blessings for each son (Genesis 49:2–27), pay close attention to the "curses" which were spoken as a result of the behaviors of some of Jacob's sons; i.e.: Reuben, Simeon, Levi.

In Genesis 49:7, the word *'cursed'* is the Hebrew word: *Arar.* It means "to bind (with a spell); to hem in with obstacles, to render powerless to resist."

In essence, Jacob rendered discipline for the actions of his two sons, Simeon and Levi, by 'hemming in their anger and wrath,' curtailing or restraining their behavior. This prophesy was fulfilled. "Levi got no inheritance except 48 towns scattered throughout different parts of Canaan. As to Simeon, they were originally given only a few towns and villages in Judah's lot" {Joshua 19:1}.

The birthright of the firstborn, Reuben, was taken from him and given to Judah because he defiled his father's bed. Reuben's succumbing to his sexual lusts stripped him and his descendants of authority and dominion. He honored his physical lusts more than his birthright, more than his eternal destiny.

In the binding or cursing of his sons, Jacob followed Father God's example as He cursed or bound Eve's childbearing process and her relationship with her husband. God cursed the ground because of Adam's obeying his wife's words instead of His.

People experiencing consequences in relationship to their behavior is also seen in the New Testament:

"Do not be deceived. God is not mocked;
for whatever a man sows, this he will also reap.
For the one who sows to his own flesh shall from
the flesh reap corruption, but the one who sows
to the Spirit shall from the Spirit reap eternal life."
Galatians 6:7–8

"For the Son of Man is going to come
in the glory of His Father
with His angels; and will then recompense every man
according to his deeds."
Matthew 16:27

Webster's explains "recompense": to "repay (a person, etc.); reward; compensate. (n): something given or done in return for something else; repayment; remuneration; something given or done to make up for a loss, injury, etc."

"each man's work will become evident; for the day will show it,
because it is to be revealed with fire; and the fire
itself will test the quality of each man's work.
If any man's work which he has built upon it remains,
he shall receive a reward."
I Corinthians 3:13–14

Read Genesis 49:28—

"All these are the twelve tribes of Israel, and this is what
their father said to them when he blessed them.

He blessed them, every one with the
blessing appropriate to him."

We can glean several 'truths' from this statement. Jacob was definitely inspired by God's Holy Spirit as he foretold or prophesied the events which would occur within each son's lineage. Jacob's sons received 'their just reward,' some good; others, not so good. Whatever was appropriate was given.

Life Application:

When we bless our children, or others, we move into the authority of speaking encouragement for obedient, responsible actions and discipline for disobedient, adverse actions. Consider this example: if our young son, David, has acted in rebellion against us, I might speak this blessing—

"David, may you obey your parents
in the Lord, for this is right.
May you honor your father and mother (which is the first
commandment with a promise),
that it may be well with you, and that
you may live long on the earth.
Ephesians 6:1–3

Friends, Cal and I agree with firm and appropriate discipline of children. This blessing would be spoken *after* suitable correction had been administered! We know God's will for David based on our knowledge of His Word. We must correct our children when they rebel or display dishonor. Understanding God's will emphasizes the enormous benefit of studying the Word and drawing close to Him. To stand in the spiritual authority or "posture" to effectively speak a blessing, we *must* be a student and a doer of the Word. Knowing God and His Word, we can "tell," announce, proclaim, *even celebrate with praise,* the things that are to come within the lives of others.

This is the key to releasing the Spoken Blessing within the lives of others: developing and maintaining a deep intimacy with God through His Spirit who lives within us.

Jacob knew what blessing was "appropriate" for each son because he was led by God's Spirit as he prophesied. I found it interesting to compare the action verb used in Genesis 49:1, "to tell" [to declare, to make known, to reveal something which one would not otherwise know, to celebrate with praise] and the action verb used in verse 28 of that chapter: "to bless," [to praise, to invoke, to ask a blessing].

If we are celebrating something we assume a certain mental and emotional posture of success, victory, authority, knowledge. Likewise, we assume a similar *spiritual posture* as we declare, announce, celebrate and bless others with the Word of God through releasing the Spoken Blessing.

As we live under the New Covenant and not the Old, we have an advantage over the Old Testament people in several ways:

1.   We have the entire Word of God, the full breadth of His revealed will, for our instruction and training;

"Every Scripture is God-breathed
(given by His inspiration) and
profitable for instruction, for reproof and conviction of sin,
for correction of error and discipline in obedience,

[and] for training in righteousness (in holy living,
in conformity to God's will in thought, purpose, and action),
so that the man of God may be complete and proficient,
well fitted and thoroughly equipped for every good work."
II Timothy 3:16–17 AMP

Releasing the Spoken Blessing into the lives, into the future of others, is a "good work."

---

2.   Living within us, we have God's Holy Spirit who shares God's revelation;

"But the Comforter (Counselor, Helper, Intercessor, Advocate,
Strengthener, Standby), the Holy Spirit, Whom the Father
will send in My name [in My place, to
represent Me and act on My behalf],
He will teach you all things.
And He will cause you to recall (will
remind you of, bring to your
remembrance) everything I have told you."
John 14:26 AMP

3.   We have access to the throne of God through our Lord Jesus, our Mediator.

"But now He has obtained a more
excellent ministry, by as much
as He is also the mediator of a better covenant, which has
been enacted on better promises.
Hebrews 8:6

"For Christ did not enter a holy place made with hands,

a mere copy of the true one, but into heaven itself,
now to appear in the presence of God for us;"
Hebrews 9:24

"Since therefore, brethren, we have confidence to enter
the holy place by the blood of Jesus, . . .
let us draw near with a sincere heart in full assurance of faith,
having our hearts sprinkled clean from an evil conscience and
our bodies washed with pure water.
Let us hold fast the confession of our hope without wavering,
for He who promised is faithful;
and let us consider how to stimulate one another
to love and good deeds,"
Hebrews 10:19, 22–24

"Stimulate," according to Webster's Dictionary means "to rouse to action or increased action, as by goading; spur on; excite." In Jacob's parting words, he deeply desired 'to rouse to action,' to urge his sons on toward their destiny with God. When we speak a blessing into someone's life, we are stimulating them to pursue their fullest potential in God's Kingdom. The focus of our blessings should be to love God, to love others and to do good deeds for His Kingdom.

Even as Egyptian slaves, Jacob's sons became a great nation. God desired for His blessing and presence to be continually experienced by these people. Moses and Aaron were instructed by God:

"Thus you shall bless the sons of Israel. You shall say to them:
'The LORD bless you, and keep you;
the LORD make His face shine on you,
and be gracious to you;
the LORD lift up His countenance on you,
and give you peace.'

> *So they shall invoke My name on the sons of*
> *Israel, and I then will bless them."*
> **Numbers 6:23–27**

Life Application:

It is very important to bless others "in the name of the Lord," because you are engaging the name that is above every name, the name of our Creator, the One who died for us; asking for His divine image to be infused into each situation. His name reflects His image. God's creation plan was for His image to be multiplied across the face of the earth.

> *" . . . The blessing of the LORD be upon you;*
> *We bless you in the name of the LORD."*
> **Psalm 129:8**

When I speak or write a blessing to someone, I end it with: "In Jesus' Name." Jesus was very clear in His instruction to us:

> *"And whatever you ask in My name,*
> *that will I do, that the Father*
> *may be glorified in the Son.*
> *If you ask Me anything in My name, I will do it."*
> **John 14:13–14**

We bless others in a manner that God would choose to bless.

Now, I realize that 'blessing' and 'asking' are two different verbs, two actions. Yet, at work here is the same principle of invoking the total character and nature of our God to operate within a person's life. When we unite our spirit with His Spirit, when we make His desire, our desire, then, whatever we ask WILL line up with or agree with His nature and character. That's why it's so important to know God intimately. We bless others in a manner that God would choose to bless.

Let's review for a moment. We have seen how God set the example of speaking life and blessings over His creation. He continued to *impart the ability to fulfill His plan* as He blessed Noah, Abram and Isaac. We read the beautiful and powerful blessing that Isaac called forth over Jacob. Continuing the heritage of the Spoken Blessing, Jacob blessed his sons. As the fulfillment of God's plan continued, Jesus followed His Father's example and explained His ways:

"Truly, truly I say to you, the Son can do nothing of Himself,
unless it is something He sees the Father
doing; for whatever the Father does,
these things the Son also does in like manner.
For the Father loves the Son, and shows Him all things that
He Himself is doing;
and greater works than these will He show Him,
that you may marvel.
For just as the Father raises the dead and gives them life,
even so the Son also gives life to whom He wishes.
John 5:19–21

Turn to Mark 10:13–16, and read about some very determined parents. Are we as determined to get our children to Jesus? Do we possess and exercise the FAITH, COMMITMENT and EXPECTATION these parents had as they refused to be denied the opportunity for their children to be blessed by Jesus? Look at what they did! Jesus' disciples tried to block their divine appointment with Jesus because they didn't perceive the children as being worthy of Jesus' time and audience. Honestly, we should learn several things here.

1. Jesus considers the lowliest of people to be worthy of His love and attention.

2. Jesus is always setting forth an example of an attitude and behavior that we are to follow "in like manner."

3. Jesus desires to bless and motivate every person to attain their destiny within God's Kingdom.

4. As believers, we are to exhibit our *faith* in Jesus, *commitment* to His goals, and *expectation* of His power and authority operating within our lives.

5. As spiritual people, we should remain humble and submissive to correction and redirection from our Lord. We must always remember that His ways are higher than our ways; His thoughts are higher than our thoughts (Isaiah 55:9).

Interestingly enough, Jesus released His faith, commitment and expectation within us, as His disciples, when He said:

> *"Truly, truly I say to you, he who believes in Me,*
> *the works that I do shall he do also;*
> *and greater works than these shall he do;*
> *because I go to the Father."*
> *"And whatever you ask in My name,*
> *that will I do, that the Father*
> *may be glorified in the Son.*
> *If you ask Me anything in My name, I will do it."*
> ***John 14:12–14***

He wants us to call upon Him, to do GREATER works than He did. I don't pronounce that in an arrogant way. I emphasize His intentions for us to walk *in* and *with* His authority, dominion and power. We must know His character. When we do, then we can speak, with confidence, His blessings upon people. And how do we know His character? We must devour His Word; we must internalize it, we must abide with Him, allowing His character to overtake our own.

"In the beginning was the Word, and the Word
was with God, and the Word was God.
He was in the beginning with God.
And the Word became flesh, and dwelt among us,
and we beheld His glory, glory as of the only begotten
from the Father, full of grace and truth."
John 1:1,2,14

We are to speak His Word, the embodiment of our Lord Jesus, as we release the Spoken Blessing into people's lives. As His Spirit lives within us, the Spirit will bring to our remembrance the Word that is *appropriate* for every situation and need. Even when we don't understand how the 'remembered' scripture relates to the person, we are to trust in His Spirit's direction, speaking His Word with confidence. We will discover that the blessing we speak will be "right on time" and "just the right fit" for that person.

WHO used the Spoken Blessing?

The Father, His Son and His Holy Spirit.

WHO should use the Spoken Blessing?

We should . . . allowing God's Spirit to speak through us.

Declare with me:

Lord, I recognize You as the
source of all my blessings.
I humble myself before You and
others to receive blessings.

I turn my heart, mind and soul towards heaven, ready to hear Your blessings for others. Teach me, Lord, to know Your voice and to heed Your instruction. I want to follow Your example of blessing others. Counsel my heart that I might know Your will. In Your precious Name, Amen.

Journal of My Journey with the Spoken Blessing

God used the Spoken Blessing to . . .

_____

_____

_____

_____

_____ .

I will use blessings to . . .

_____

_____

_____

_____ .

As I speak blessings over others, I expect . . .

_____

_____

_____

_____

_____ .

I will ask God's Spirit to show me . . .

_____

_____

_____
_____
_____.

I will follow the example of Jesus when He . . .

_____
_____
_____
_____
_____.

Write a blessing to help someone's heart change from 'bitter' to 'better.'

_____
_____
_____
_____
_____
_____
_____.

*"A joyful heart makes a cheerful face, but when
the heart is sad, the spirit is broken."*
Proverbs 15:13

Chapter 2

What is the Basis for the Spoken Blessing?

The Spoken Blessing is founded upon God's
1.   commitment to His creation
2.   commitment to His covenant
3.   commitment to His name, His nature, His image.

"Then God spoke to Noah and to his sons with him saying,
'Now behold, I Myself do establish My covenant with you,
and with your descendants after you;
and with every living creature that is with you;
the birds, the cattle, and every beast of the earth with you;
of all that comes out of the ark, even every beast of the earth.
And I will establish My covenant with you;
and all flesh shall never again be cut
off by the water of the flood,
neither shall there again be a flood to destroy the earth.'
'. . . . and I will remember My covenant,
which is between Me and you
and every living creature of all flesh; and never again shall
the water become a flood to destroy all flesh.'"
Genesis 9:8–11,15

    God showed a commitment to His creation by blessing them. We reviewed this in the first chapter (Genesis 1:21–22, 26–31). He called upon Himself, the fullness of the Godhead;

God, the Father; God, the Son; God, the Holy Spirit; to help and assist their creation.

In God's instruction to His people, He commanded certain ways of dealing with others and with Himself. Keep in mind, that whatever God expected of His people, He would perform no less. If He recognized that 'taking an oath' or 'making a vow' created a binding obligation (Numbers 30:1–2), then He would place the same or stricter requirement upon Himself. We were created in His image.

> *"When you make a vow to the LORD your God,*
> *you shall not delay to pay it,*
> *for it would be sin in you,*
> *and the LORD your God will surely require it of you.*
> *You shall be careful to perform what goes out from your lips,*
> *just as you have voluntarily vowed to the LORD your God,*
> *what you have promised."*
> **Deuteronomy 23:21,23**

In past days, when a person made a vow, a solemn promise or pledge, to the Lord, they were to be prompt to pay it. Likewise, the Lord placed the same requirements of promptness and commitment upon Himself. His people were admonished to perform what goes out from their lips. He did, also. Male and female were created in His image. Therefore, if God wanted mankind to act in this or that way, He would do the same, because, He was the *original* Being from which the images were made.

Side note: Read in verse 6 of Genesis 9 that anyone who sheds the blood of another, will have his own blood shed BECAUSE that act attacks the IMAGE of God.

Even when God felt it necessary to purge the earth and judge mankind for their flagrant sinfulness, He preserved man, His creatures and His world; continuing His commitment to His creation. After the Flood, God was quick to reaffirm His covenant with Noah and his sons:

"And God blessed Noah and his sons and said to them,
'Be fruitful and multiply, and fill the earth.
And as for you, be fruitful and multiply;
populate the earth abundantly and multiply in it.'"
Genesis 9:1,7

"And God said, 'This is the sign of the covenant which I am
making between Me and you and every living creature that is
with you, for all successive generations;
I set My bow in the cloud, and it shall be for a sign
of a covenant between Me and the earth.
And it shall come about, when I bring a cloud over the earth,
that the bow shall be seen in the cloud,
and I will remember My covenant,
which is between Me and you
and every living creature of all flesh; and never again
shall the water become a flood to destroy all flesh.'"
Genesis 9:12–15

God established an eternal covenant with mankind and with every living creature. He confirmed a covenant that He would always remember *"for all successive generations."* Following Noah's *'successive generations,'* we discover that the Lord instructed a man to "think outside the box;" to "color outside the lines." God challenged this man to go beyond what he could see or imagine.

"Now the Lord said to Abram,
'Go forth from your country, and from your relatives
and from your father's house, to the land which I will show you;
and I will make you a great nation, and I will bless you,
*and make your name great; and so you shall be a **blessing**;*
{Blessing—*Brakah:* benefit, favor, peace,
a gift or present to gain goodwill}
and I will bless those who bless you,

and the one who curses you I will curse.
And in you all the families of the earth shall be blessed.'"
Genesis 12:1–3

Doesn't that last phrase: *"and in you all the families of the earth shall be blessed,"* reflect God's covenant promise with Noah: *"for all successive generations?"* Abram was a recipient of Noah's blessing from God, but, it didn't stop with him. God declared it, thus, He caused it to happen. Blessings flowed through Abram onto others. *God established the pattern for releasing the Spoken Blessing: an ever-continuing ripple effect.*

In Genesis 17:1–9, God carefully identified the covenant responsibilities of both parties: Himself and Abram. Make note of God's part and Abram's part; the longevity of both.

"Now when Abram was ninety-nine years old, the LORD
appeared to Abram and said to him,
'I am God Almighty; walk before Me, and be blameless.
And I will establish My covenant between Me and you,
and I will multiply you exceedingly.'
And Abram fell on his face, and God talked with him, saying,
'As for Me, behold, My covenant is with you,
and you shall be the father of a multitude of nations.
No longer shall your name be called Abram,
but your name shall be Abraham;
for I will make you the father of a multitude of nations.
And I will make you exceedingly fruitful,
and I will make nations of you, and kings shall
come forth from you.
And I will establish My covenant between Me and you
and your descendants after you throughout their
generations for an everlasting covenant, to be God
to you and to your descendants after you.
And I will give to you and to your descendants after you,
the land of your sojournings, all the land of Canaan,

for an everlasting possession;
and I will be their God.'
God said further to Abraham, 'Now as for you, you shall
keep My covenant, you and your descendants after you
throughout their generations.'"

Father God's commitment to His covenant continued to be upheld throughout the generations. And in the 'fullness of time,' God's promised Messiah, Savior, Redeemer, was brought into the world.

"But when the fulness of the time came, God sent forth His Son,
born of a woman, born under the Law,
in order that He might redeem those who were under the Law,
that we might receive the adoption as sons.
And because you are sons, God has sent
forth the Spirit of His Son
into our hearts, crying, 'Abba, Father!'
Therefore you are no longer a slave, but a son; and if a son,
then an heir through God."
Galatians 4:4–7

Jesus brought with Him a new and better covenant through the shedding of His blood on Calvary. His cross became the 'sign of remembrance' for the New Covenant.

In Luke 22:20, we read:

"And in the same way He took the cup
after they had eaten saying,
'This cup which is poured out for you is
the new covenant in My blood.'"

II Corinthians 3:4–6 continues to describe our new covenant:

"And such confidence we have through Christ toward God.
*Not that we are **adequate** in ourselves*
to consider anything as coming from ourselves,
*but our **adequacy** is from God,*
*who also made us adequate as **servants** of a new covenant,*
not of the letter, but of the Spirit; for the letter kills,
but the Spirit gives life."

This is a true and accurate description of the ministry of the Spirit as we speak blessings upon others. We are *not* adequate, we are *not* sufficient enough to accomplish this work by ourselves. Our adequacy IS from God. His grace is sufficient for us, enabling us to achieve the desired end. We desire to release into other's lives: life, hope, love for the Lord and a fulfillment of their destiny. We are servants of the new and better covenant, executing our King's decree. Just as messengers personally carried the King's word, near and far, to his subjects; we carry forth our King's message which is expressed through His Word.

As you begin a life of speaking blessings over people, they will associate you with one who brings 'glad tidings,' which encourage, uplift and transform their lives.

Through the power and presence of His Spirit living within us, empowering us to release His Word, we can speak life, not death, into our fellow servants. As you begin a life of speaking blessings over people, they will associate you with one who brings 'glad tidings,' which encourage, uplift and transform their lives. They will receive your blessings as one who has run a long, hot race and needs a bucket of cool, refreshing water poured over them. That hot and weary soul is noticeably revived by the water flowing over them. I have even watched runners tilt their heads and mouths upward, attempting to drink some of the water. A recovery occurs within that runner. A restoration begins. A body is renewed.

Keep this visual image in your mind as you set out to carry your King's message; as you begin to speak blessings over people. You will experience this very thing! It is so thrilling to be the pourer of that life-giving water! Speaking blessings will become a delight to you and to your Lord.

May I highlight something here:

For many years, I lived my life as a believer without grasping the truth, nor experiencing the reality of God's Spirit living within me. He had been there, ever since I had accepted Jesus as my Savior, yet, I didn't mentally or spiritually comprehend this fact. Over the years, I recognized a deep yearning within which needed to be satisfied. As I searched for fulfillment, I discovered God's treasure tucked inside of me. Wanting to know Jesus in a deeper, more powerful way, I submitted more and more of my SELF to the teaching and leading of His Spirit. Then, I experienced His perfecting the nature and character of the Lord Jesus within me. When we accept the free gift of salvation from Jesus, we have the promise of His Holy Spirit living within us (John 14:16–17, 26; Acts 1:8; I Corinthians 12:12–13).

Consider the following analogy of the presence of God's Holy Spirit within our lives:

I receive notice that a wealthy relative has bequeathed to me his beautiful home. I have a choice to accept or decline this gift. I choose to accept. As I am handed the keys to this elaborate house, the officiator of the will explains something—there is a permanent resident, a respected guest, who lives in the house. He will offer his help and friendship as often or as much as I permit. The choice of developing the friendship is mine. As I "test the waters" of this friendship, I discover the joy of getting to know this guest. As I encounter the challenges of life, I go to him for help and counsel. Interestingly, he is always willing to assist me. His wisdom is far greater than mine. Our friendship develops into one in which I am eager to spend time with him every day. I need our times together. His advice—his words— encourage and strengthen me, preparing me for the responsibilities of every day. I invite him to accompany me throughout my day. He's such a comfort to me. We walk and talk together. I share my heart with him. He shares his with me. There comes a time in my life in which my desires begin reflecting his. Seeing the future through his eyes becomes an important goal for me. I want what he wants.

As we give God's Spirit more room to operate within our submitted lives, the greater influence and effect He has within us. Our life matures to the point where we can offer encouragement, truth and peace to others. The Kingdom of God is present within a life that is submitted to God. Our life is all about expanding and encouraging the furtherance of His Kingdom within the hearts and lives of others.

II Corinthians 4:6, 7 explains God's promised treasure, His Spirit:

"For God, who said, 'Light shall shine out of darkness,'
is the One who has shone in our hearts to give the light of the
knowledge of the glory of God in the face of Christ.
But we have this treasure in earthen vessels,
that the surpassing
greatness of the power may be of God
and not from ourselves."

God desires for His people to have His nature which emanates power, confidence and peace to infill and cloth them once again, as they had in the Garden, before sin entered.

"And the man and his wife were both naked and not ashamed."
Genesis 2:25

When verse 25 identified that Adam and Eve were 'not ashamed,' it referred to their feeling secure and safe; not susceptible to evil. They did not feel danger. They were innocent, pure and, thus, transparent.

Then sin entered their hearts and lives. They lost their sense of peace and security. They were humiliated, feeling exposed and vulnerable. They felt a need to cover themselves.

"Then the eyes of both of them were opened,
and they knew that they were naked;
and they sewed fig leaves together and
made themselves loin coverings."
Genesis 3:7

King David declared and rejoiced over God's covering him with His nature, His glory, which provided protection, provision and deliverance. David looked to God as the One who had the ability and desire to restore him to his ordained position and authority as king.

"But Thou, O Lord, art a shield about me,
My glory, and the One who lifts my head."
Psalm 3:3

The word, *glory,* denotes God's weight, honor, majesty, abundance and wealth. "Lifting someone's head" makes reference to God's ability and desire to restore us to our previous position that mankind knew in the Garden of Eden. We can, once again, walk and talk with God in the cool of the day (Genesis 3:8). Once again, we can operate with the authority and dominion that God, originally, gave to Adam and Eve (Genesis 1:28).

Pay close attention to something notated in the first two verses of Psalm 3:

"O LORD, how my adversaries have increased!

Many are rising up against me.
Many are saying of my soul,
'There is no deliverance for him in God.'"

King David had fled for his life in the face of a rebellious, scheming son, Absalom. At least 20,000 men had aligned themselves with Absalom to war against the king—20,000 people bent on his destruction. That had David's attention and focus.

Life Application:

We will encounter people who are focusing on their "woes" of life. When you hear about their challenges, you might understand their concerns. Certainly extend a compassionate heart, but do not encourage them to wallow in their "woes." Redirect their focus to their Deliverer, their Provider, their Strength and their Shield.

Draw from the power of the Word and bless them, by proclaiming:

"May the Lord be your Strength and your
Salvation. Whom shall you fear?
No one! May you feel the presence and power of Almighty God
as He sends His angels to be in charge concerning your ways.
May you always remember that He will never leave you
or forsake you.
May you know, for certain, that God has great plans
for you, not for calamity, but for a future, full of hope.
May He direct your steps along the pathway of life.
May you draw close to Him and He will draw near to you.
In Jesus' Name, Amen."

The Spoken Blessing is based on:

- God's commitment to His **creation**
- His commitment to His **covenant**
- His commitment to His **name and nature.**

"Turn to Me, and be saved, all the ends of the earth;
For I am God, and there is no other.
I have sworn by Myself,
The word has gone forth from My mouth in righteousness
And will not turn back,
That to Me every knee will bow,
every tongue will swear allegiance."
Isaiah 45:22–23

The meaning of the Hebrew word for **sworn**, *shaba,* gives us insight into the totality and holiness of God's name and nature. *Shaba* means "to complete [seven], to swear, to confirm with an oath, to pledge allegiance to God with an oath. *Sheba* or *shibah* means "seven." The number seven was sacred. Oaths were confirmed by seven sacrifices, or by seven witnesses or seven pledges.

Swearing was the giving of one's unbreakable word that he would faithfully perform a promised deed or that he would not harm his partner. God used this human convention on occasion. Since there was no higher authority than Himself, He swore by Himself or by His holiness.

" . . . By Myself I have sworn, declares the LORD,
because you have done this thing,
and have not withheld your son, your only son,
indeed I will greatly bless you,
and I will greatly multiply your seed as the stars of the heavens,
and as the sand which is on the seashore;
and your seed shall possess the gate of their enemies.
And in your seed all the nations of the earth shall be blessed,
because you have obeyed My voice."

Genesis 22:16–18

God swore by Himself to bless Abraham and to greatly multiply Abraham's descendants. God indicated that the fulfillment of Abraham's blessing was dependent upon Himself: His nature, His power, His resources and was related to Abram's obedience.

This fact reminds me of the activity of God as noted in Psalm 17:3:

> " . . . Thou hast **visited** me by night . . . "

Visited refers to an action on the part of God which produces a beneficial result for His people.

This scripture offers me reassurance of God's faithfully working within my life and within the lives of others. Several years ago, I was impressed by God's Spirit to speak a specific blessing over our daughter, Elizabeth. I spoke this blessing over her the entire school year.

> *"May you be confident of this very thing,*
> *that God will complete and perfect the*
> *good work He has begun in you*
> *until the day of Jesus Christ."*
> **Philippians 1:6**

I was to set the example of trusting God to be interested and ACTIVE within her life. Years later, as a young woman, Elizabeth is confident that God has an answer for her challenges and a creative solution for her dilemmas. If others observe our trust in God through our words and actions, they are more likely to do the same. We, as believers, are constantly being watched. Do we live a life that expresses confidence in our God to be steadfast to His covenant people? Or, are our words and actions indicative of FEAR, DOUBT and UNBELIEF?

Sometimes, there are opportunities for correction in someone's outlook. Sometimes, it's mine that needs correcting. A few years ago, I was being stretched beyond my 'comfort zone:' physically, mentally, spiritually and emotionally. In exasperation, I exclaimed: "There are not enough hours in the day for me to do ALL that I have to do!" Just as thunder rumbles loudly across the sky, God's voice vibrated within me: "Ann, you have just cursed yourself. You definitely won't have time to do it all because you have bound My hand from helping you. You have limited My blessing you. Take your eyes off of yourself and your circumstances and place them on Me and My abundant provision." It didn't take long for me to repent, to call those word curses 'null and void,' and to confess God's blessings: supplying all my needs according to His riches in glory through Christ Jesus!

Recently, one of our children was preparing for a college entrance exam and asked me to pray. He explained his perception of this test: "The outcome of this exam will determine my future!" My response to that was: "No, a test does not control your future, only God does." Then, I followed that correction with a blessing:

*"May the Lord cause you to prosper
and excel in all that you do.
May His Spirit highlight those things that you need to know.
May He bring to your remembrance all
the facts, figures, and formulas
that are needed to complete this test.
May the peace of our Lord Jesus guard
your heart and your mind.
May you call upon Him and He will answer you.
In Jesus' Name, Amen."*

The preceding blessing exemplifies our Life Application.

Life Application:

If you were to search the Scriptures for that specific blessing, you would not find it. Many times, I base my blessings on the *principles* found within the Word and on the *character* and *operation* of the Holy Trinity. I know that God desires for us to "prosper and excel" in all that we do because I have read the story about Joseph as he served Potiphar, an Egyptian officer of Pharoah (Genesis 39:1–6).

"Now Joseph had been taken down to Egypt; and Potiphar,
an Egyptian officer of Pharaoh, the captain of the bodyguard,
bought him from the Ishmaelites, who
had taken him down there.
And the LORD was with Joseph, so he
became a successful man.
And he was in the house of his master, the Egyptian.
Now his master saw that the LORD was with him and how the
LORD caused all that he did to prosper in his hand.
So Joseph found favor in his sight, and became his personal
servant; and he made him overseer over his house,
and all that he owned he put in his charge.
And it came about that from the time he made him overseer in
his house, and over all that he owned, the LORD blessed
the Egyptian's house on account of Joseph,
thus the LORD's blessing was upon all that he owned,
in the house and in the field.
So he left everything he owned in Joseph's charge;
and with him there he did not concern himself with anything,
except food which he ate."

I integrated that principle of God's blessing His people into my perception of Him and His activity. Secondly, as I have grown in my understanding and experience with God's Spirit, I have recognized the consistent way He teaches, trains, informs and reminds me of things I need to know and/or do. This agrees with the scripture in which Jesus explained the promise and the purpose of His Spirit.

"But the Helper, the Holy Spirit, whom
the Father will send in My name,
He will teach you all things, and bring to your remembrance
all that I said to you.
Peace I leave with you; My peace I give
to you; not as the world gives,
do I give to you. Let not your heart be
troubled, nor let it be fearful."
John 14:26–27

God honors His word to people. He upholds His integrity and honor by performing whatever He agreed to within a covenant. We do have a 'better covenant' with God through His Son, Jesus Christ. Remember: God operated within a human custom as He swore by Himself to fulfill His promise to Abraham to give us strong encouragement and hope in Him and in the unchangeableness of His purpose (Hebrews 6:13–19). Through God, we can expect to obtain every good thing. We can help others in grasping and applying this hope, this assurance of God's faithfulness to them, as we speak blessings into their lives.

His truth must become 'the anchor of their soul.'

Recently, the Lord directed me to write a set of blessings entitled: "Hope: The Anchor of the Soul." {This blessing set is listed under Resources.} God impressed me with people's deep need for HOPE. Remember, HOPE refers to a desire of some good thing with the expectation of obtaining it. He showed me that many people, including myself, have grown up hearing: "Well, honey, I don't want you to get your hopes up." People have said that to me throughout my life, under the pretense of comforting me. But, in reality, it served to confine me to a state of depression and *loss* of hope. Honestly, that statement undermines one's ability to expect their desire to be fulfilled. It is counterproductive to true HOPE.

Many people have dared to hope for something and have been disappointed and hurt. One of the problems with our hope is that it is often focused on someone or something to fulfill that need. Our focus must be redirected to God. He is the Supplier of every need. He is our Good Shepherd, we shall have no want (Psalm 23:1).

I bless others with HOPE that their faithful God will supply all their needs according to His riches in glory in Christ Jesus (Philippians 4:19). In my blessing, I remind them that God is able to make all grace abound to them, having all sufficiency in everything, enabling them to accomplish every good deed (II Corinthians 9:8). Do you see how HOPE can be built and encouraged as you release such a blessing?!

That blessing of hope and encouragement can flow both ways. We can *sow* blessings into the soil of another's heart and personally *reap* God's benefits. II Corinthians 9:10–11 explains:

"Now He who supplies seed to the sower
and bread for food, will supply
and multiply your seed for sowing and increase the harvest
of your righteousness;
you will be enriched in everything for all liberality, which
is producing thanksgiving to God."

Notice several consequences of sowing seeds of God's blessings:

1.   The harvest of your righteousness will be increased (indicating success in being fruitful and multiplying).

Personally, I have received many testimonies of how the Spoken Blessing has impacted people's lives: their confidence has been revived, their friends have accepted Jesus as their Savior, thoughts of suicide have been overcome, negative attitudes have been exchanged for an excitement for life and expectations for good things to happen.

Cal and I are observing, with great delight and awe, how God has multiplied and nurtured the seeds of compassion and generosity that we have sown within our four children. Our children express God's compassion and help in different ways, yet the 'fruit' is recognizable. God continues to provide Cal and me with more opportunities, more seed for sowing His blessings.

2.   Your liberality and good deeds will be enhanced and increased because you have been enriched.

Cal and I always ask God to increase our abilities and wisdom as we give and do for others.

3.   Others will offer thanksgiving to God as a result of your liberality and good deeds.

As we bless others, their focus is directed to God and to their trusting and thanking Him "to do exceeding abundantly beyond all that they ask or think, according to the power that works within them," (Ephesians 3:20).

The blessing of God is eternal. His commitment to His creation, His covenant, His holy name and nature, is forever and everlasting. This foundational truth must sink down into your soul: your mind, will and emotions. This understanding is vital to your ability and confidence in speaking and receiving the Spoken Blessing. Speak and release a blessing over someone, today.

This is my blessing for you:

May you know God as the great, I AM.
May He become everything to you.
May you love Him with all your
heart, soul, mind and strength.
May you love your neighbor as yourself.
May you look for opportunities to bless others.
May God's Holy Spirit give you boldness to declare
His Word over others. May they receive the Spoken
Blessing with joy and hope for their future.
May you give thanksgiving to God
for His steadfast love.
In Jesus' Name, Amen.

Journal of My Journey with the Spoken Blessing

I am confident that God wants to bless His creation because . . .

_____

_____

_____

_____

_____ .

I know God as a "covenant-keeping" God by His . . .

_____

_____

_____

_____

_____ .

I am not adequate by myself to bless others, but with . . .

_____

_____

_____

_____

_____ .

I will help to redirect someone's focus back to God by . . .

_____

_____

_____

_____

_____ .

I have witnessed God's activity in my life when He . . .

_____

_____

_____

_____ .

Write a blessing for someone who is struggling with a situation.

_____

_____

_____

_____

_____

_____

_____ .

"Anxiety in the heart of man weighs it down,
But a good word makes it glad."
Proverbs 12:25

Chapter 3

When is the Spoken Blessing Given?

Most of us recognize the importance of "timing" within the natural and supernatural worlds. The saying goes: "Timing is everything." Young children learn when not to interrupt Daddy's activity and when to obey Mommy as they get that "look" from her. Throughout our daily lives, "timing" is essential to accomplish our tasks. If we need to ask a favor or want to give a gift, we carefully consider "when" to do it.

Ecclesiastes 3:1 identifies:

> *"To everything there is a season,*
> *and a time to every purpose*
> *under the heaven:" KJV*

Season stems from a word that means: to be determined, to be appointed, to be fixed. It refers to an appointed time or times. *Time* relates to the right time, the proper time, a season or a short-lived season. There are three principle situations which the word, *time,* describes:

1.   regular events
2.   the appropriate time for a nonrecurring incident
3.   a set time.

The Greek equivalent for "time" used in the New Testament is *kairos. Kairos* implies that which time gives an opportunity to do. It implies not the convenience of the season, but the necessity of the *task at hand*—whether the time provides a good, convenient opportunity or not.

Purpose signifies pleasure, delight, wish, desire; a matter, business, or pursuit. Isaiah 53:10 states that God's delight or good pleasure will prosper in the hand of the Messiah.

Will God's *purpose* **prosper** in our hands?

Our spiritual posture, at this point, is one of submission.

We must ask our Father's pleasure and desire as we prepare to bless others. What does He want to accomplish in that person's life? What pursuit can we encourage as we release blessings into their life? Our spiritual posture, at this point, is one of submission. This type of submission is depicted in the familiar pictures of Jesus sitting on the ground next to a large rock. His hands are clasped, resting on the rock—His eyes and face are focused on the heavens. Jesus constantly submitted Himself to His Father asking for His will to be made known. Then, in obedience, He responded (Luke 6:12–13). We must ask His Spirit to bring to our remembrance His Word that will reflect His will. Recall in Genesis 49:28, concerning the blessing of Jacob's sons: *"He blessed them, every one with the blessing appropriate to him."* As we are the Lord's representatives, we must be sensitive to His timing and purpose for releasing a Spoken Blessing. There is a *task at hand* to be accomplished:

> *". . . we are ambassadors for Christ, as*
> *though God were entreating*
> *through us; we beg you on behalf of Christ,*
> *be reconciled to God."*
> ***II Corinthians 5:20***

Our task is assisting in the reconciliation and restoration

of people to God through introducing them to Christ or to read-justing their focus to Christ. The Spoken Blessing is a tool we can use to accomplish this task. There will be occasions when you feel the need to correct or redirect someone as you bless them:

*"May you not continue to call this day
"bad," but call it "good,"
for the Word of the Lord says:
'This is the day that the Lord has made,
I will rejoice and be glad in it.'
May you not look upon your days with sorrow, but with joy,
rejoicing that the Lord has declared
that He will never leave you
nor forsake you."*

As you speak this blessing, the hearer will likely assume an attitude of repentance. They may nod their heads or verbally respond: "Yes, Lord. I'm sorry. It is a good day." You would continue to bless them:

*"May you gain wisdom from your past and approach
your future with a new attitude and outlook.
May your eyes be focused on the author and finisher of your
faith, Lord Jesus. May you focus your face like flint on Him
as He beckons you to walk on the water;
to step out of your comfort zone,
relying totally on Him.
May you not lean on your own understanding,
but trust in Him.
In Jesus' Name, Amen."*

In that blessing, you have presented them with a need for repentance by speaking the truth of God's Word in love. You have redirected their thoughts to the Truth which will liberate and edify them. You have encouraged them to submit their lives and future to the authority and faithfulness of our Lord Jesus. In essence, you have accomplished the *task at hand.* In doing so, you have followed the example of Jesus found in Matthew 4:17, (AMP):

> *"From that time Jesus began to preach, crying out*
> *'Repent [change your mind for the better,*
> *heartily amend your ways, with abhorrence of your past sins],*
> *for the kingdom of heaven is at hand.'"*

"The kingdom of heaven" and the *"the kingdom of God"* are interchangeable phrases. Spiritually, the kingdom of God is within the human heart; within the heart that has been humbled and receptive to God's authority and control.

Consider the definition of *heaven:* aloft, the sky, height, heaven (s). There are two main categories:

1. the physical heavens with differing locations
2. where God lives.

The Spoken Blessing can address the physical world and the spiritual world in which a person lives. I have spoken this blessing over our adult sons who play softball:

> *"May God give you the strength to run,*
> *the discernment for which*
> *ball to hit and the accuracy to 'field' the ball.*
> *May His angels be set in charge concerning all your ways.*
> *May your conduct be such as to glorify your heavenly Father.*
> *May you have victory.*
> *In Jesus' Name, Amen."*

Is it wrong to bless others in such ordinary events such as playing softball? No! God desires for us to prosper and excel in ALL that we do! God set the example for us as I discussed in Chapter 2. Let's review Genesis 39:3:

"Now his master saw that the LORD was with him and how the LORD caused all that he did to prosper in his hand."

. . . Heaven touched Earth for supernatural purposes.

The things that Joseph accomplished for Potiphar were in the natural, physical realm. Yet, Heaven touched Earth for supernatural purposes. The Lord's perfect "timing" is emphasized throughout the story of Joseph being sold into slavery, purchased by Potiphar, used and abused as a slave, then promoted to a position of great authority, power and influence. Joseph gained respect from unbelievers.

Speaking of "time," we must commit ourselves to take the TIME to speak blessings into people's lives. Be alert to the events in people's lives which cause them stress, concern, joy and excitement. Be sensitive and responsive to their specific interests. As you personalize a blessing to their need, they will listen and receive it. The potential of our sons' "softball playing" blessing was that it:

1.   Reinforced that God was so personal that He was interested in the 'little' things that were significant to them.
      Our Big, Big God is sincerely interested in the little, little concerns of our lives.

2.   Focused their attention to "from whence cometh my help . . ." God would be acknowledged as they succeed in their sport.
      "I will lift up my eyes to the mountains; from whence shall my help come?

> *My help comes from the LORD, who made heaven and earth."* (Psalm 121:1,2).

3.   Provided an opportunity to tell others about God's favor and grace that surrounded them.

> *Anthony, our oldest son, was injured on the softball field. Painfully lying on the ground, he testified to a friend about God's miraculous healing of his heart when he was seven and that he trusted God to heal him, again. Our friend was deeply touched by God's mercy and, subsequently, honored God as she shared her own testimony of the Lord's healing power. What the enemy meant for harm, God allowed for good. His name was glorified and sanctified. Anthony's back was restored within two weeks. He was victorious through Christ!*

4.   Drew the attention of others towards the Lord's favor (Genesis 39:3).

> *As our friend described the circumstances concerning Anthony's softball injury, she honored the Lord for all that He had done in our lives, recognizing His steadfast favor that rested upon us.*

5.   Encouraged me in my faith, that God cares for my children and assists them in all their ways:

> *"So faith comes by hearing and hearing by the Word of Christ"* (Romans 10:17).

> *God reassured me that when I can't be there for my children, especially in a time of need, He will send someone to assist them. Our friend was there to pray for and comfort Anthony.*

Softball games are "regular events" in the context of the definition of 'time.' Let's consider other "regular events:"

The Spoken Blessing in Other Regular Events

1. **Attending school: Relationships, reports, tests, try-outs, etc. can be blessed.**
    Consider the principle described in Proverbs 20:11

"It is by his deeds that a lad distinguishes himself if his conduct is pure and right."

and translate it into a Spoken Blessing:

"May your thoughts, actions and words be pure and right. May they set you apart from others."

Consider Daniel 1:17

"And as for these four youths, God gave them knowledge and intelligence in every branch of literature and wisdom; Daniel even understood all kinds of visions and dreams."

and compose a blessing with it:

"May God give you wisdom, knowledge and understanding in every area of your education. May He give you revelation in visions, dreams and in the supernatural. May you always give God the glory for your abilities. In Jesus' Name, Amen."

In Daniel 2:19–23, carefully read Daniel's response to God after the Lord honored his request for help:

"Then the mystery was revealed to Daniel in a night vision. Then Daniel blessed the God of heaven;

Daniel answered and said,
'Let the name of God be blessed forever and ever,
for wisdom and power belong to Him.
And it is He who changes the times and the epochs;
He removes kings and establishes kings;
He gives wisdom to wise men,
and knowledge to men of understanding.
It is He who reveals the profound and hidden things;
He knows what is in the darkness,
and the light dwells with Him.
To Thee, O God of my fathers, I give thanks and praise,
for Thou hast given me wisdom and power;
even now Thou hast made known to me
what we requested of Thee,
for Thou has made known to us the king's matter.'"

Encouraging this submissive and awe-filled attitude towards God is a primary goal of releasing the blessing over people.

The fact that Daniel blessed the name of the Lord is noteworthy. It indicates a humble attitude, one filled with respect, submission and recognition of God's supreme dominion and authority over Daniel's life and over those around him. Encouraging this submissive and awe-filled attitude towards God is a primary goal of releasing the blessing over people. When the cares of life challenge people, we can direct their focus to the One who knows everything and has an answer for all situations. We can help build their confidence to the level that Daniel possessed.

Meditating or thinking about God's goodness and mercy is an important spiritual activity to develop.

Daniel blessed the name of the Lord. We can set this example as we ask our children how the Lord worked good things in their day. Meditating or thinking about God's goodness and mercy is an important spiritual activity to develop. When your children describe God's activity in their lives, begin to bless Him for being their Provider, their Healer, their Protector, their Faithful Friend. This should be an ongoing process of learning how to honor God, His nature and His name.

When I pray and bless people at our church, I ask them to report to me of how God has responded to their need. Many do. Together, we glorify God and thank Him for His loving-kindness. We are both encouraged 'to not grow weary of well doing.' Our praise and thanksgiving sanctifies God in our lives. We set Him apart as the One to receive ALL honor and glory!

Relationships can be blessed:

"May the Lord provide a friend for you as
He did for Jonathan and David.
May your friendship be based on love and commitment,
preferring the other over yourself.
May you serve to encourage one another.
May you uphold and honor the reputation of each other.
May you, both, be upright and faithful to the Lord.
I Samuel 19:1–7; 20:1–23

I would encourage you to read all of chapters 19 and 20 in I Samuel. Consider the dynamics of the situation and the unselfish love that was shown. Jonathan spoke a blessing over David in 20:13b.

2.   **Working 9 to 5: This "regular event" encompasses a large majority of the adult population.**
One of my favorite blessings to speak over fellow believers is found in Ruth 2:12—

> *"May the LORD reward your work, and your wages be full from the LORD, the God of Israel, under whose wings you have come to seek refuge."*

Remember that Deuteronomy 28 identifies the extensiveness of God's blessings for His people. This includes our careers and working environment:

> *"Blessed shall you be in the city, and blessed shall you be in the country."*
> ***Verse 3***

Deuteronomy 8:18 reminds us that God is committed to upholding His covenant, which translates into financially supporting and strengthening His people:

> *"But you shall remember the LORD your God, for it is He who is giving you power to make wealth, that He may confirm His covenant which He swore to your fathers, as it is this day."*

Using this verse and foundational truth, a blessing can be spoken:

> *"May you always remember the Lord your God, for it is He who gives you power to make wealth. May His faithfulness to you confirm His covenant that*

He established with His people over the generations.
In Jesus' Name, Amen."

As we discovered in Chapter 2, God is committed to His creation, His covenant, His name and nature. I am not promoting a "get rich" scheme. I am proclaiming the truths that are in God's Word. Here's another blessing concerning 'wealth' or money:

"May you bring the whole tithe into the storehouse,
so that there may be food in God's house.
May you prove to yourself that God is true to His Word,
that as you give Him a tenth of all your earnings,
you will see Him open the windows of heaven and pour out
for you a blessing until it overflows.
May you know the Lord as your Good Shepherd,
for you shall have no want.
In Jesus' Name, Amen."
Malachi 3:10; Psalm 23:1

We are to request and accept the *whole* counsel of the Lord. We are not to 'cut and 'paste' the verses we like, discarding those that challenge us or, even, correct us. Tithing, returning to the Lord a tenth of our total earnings, is vital to our experiencing the fullness of God's blessings. Being faithful to give gifts and offerings is a component part to our being generous. As we give to others, we are giving to the Lord. He declared it:

"Then the righteous will answer Him, saying,
'Lord, when did we see You hungry, and feed You, or thirsty,
and give You drink? And when did we see You a stranger,
and invite You in, or naked, and clothe You?
And when did we see You sick, or in prison, and come to You?'
And the King will answer and say to them,
'Truly I say to you, to the extent that you did it

> *to one of these brothers of Mine, even the*
> *least of them, you did it to Me.'"*
> **Matthew 25:37–40**

We are to receive God's Word for our own lives and impart these truths to others. We can do this through using the Spoken Blessing. Our faith should not be expressed only in our traditional Sunday worship services. Our faith should be seen within our daily lives in the way we conduct ourselves and in how we relate to others: our God, our family, our co-workers, our neighbors. The Book of Ruth provides several excellent examples of people living out their faith in the presence of others.

In Ruth 1:4, we determine that Naomi lived with her two sons and their Moabite wives for ten years in the land of Moab. After the death of both sons, Naomi decided to return to Bethlehem, accompanied by her two daughters-in-law. In Ruth 1:8–9, Naomi encouraged these women to return to Moab and spoke a blessing over them, calling upon the covenant name of God to bless them:

> *"May the LORD deal kindly with you as you have dealt*
> *with the dead and with me.*
> *May the LORD grant that you may find rest,*
> *each in the house of her husband."*

Naomi would not have used the covenant name of God if she knew her daughters-in-law would not have understood it. When we speak to someone, we employ words and terms that they understand. The purpose of communication is to exchange information. Therefore, it would be safe to assume that Naomi had lived a life of faith before her daughters-in-law during those ten years. Ruth 1:16–17 identifies the positive influence her faith had on one of these women.

"But Ruth said, 'Do not urge me to leave you or turn back from
following you; for where you go, I will go,
and where you lodge, I will lodge.
Your people shall be my people,
and your God, my God.
Where you die, I will die, and there I will be buried.
Thus may the LORD do to me and worse,
if anything but death parts you and me.'"

Your life touches others.

Walking out our faith, day after day, can have a similar influence on people. During the 40+ hours each week that you spend at work, you have great potential for imparting your faith to others. You can release blessings over people within your work environment as Boaz did in his:

"Now behold, Boaz came from Bethlehem
and said to the reapers,
'May the LORD be with you.' And they said to him,
'May the LORD bless you. .'"
Ruth 2:4

Cal and I own and operate Hellen's Uniform Shop located in Tallahassee, Florida. Within our store, we take the liberty to pray for and bless our customers. We encourage our employees to do the same. It is not unusual for our customers, for whom we have prayed or blessed, to return and share how God moved on their behalf. We have the privilege of rejoicing with them, thanking God for His mercy and grace.

Beloved reader, *you* have a sphere of influence whether your work is within your home, or within the classroom of your child (as a volunteer), within your neighborhood, your business, your recreational activities, etc. Your life touches others. What impression will you leave on them?

3.   Attending weekly worship services:
Every believer has a responsibility to edify and build up one another.

We are to be equipped *"for the work of service to the building up of the body of Christ. . . ."*

WHEN and for HOW LONG . . .

"until we all attain to the unity of the faith,
and of the knowledge of the Son of God, to a mature man,
to the measure of the stature which
belongs to the fulness of Christ. "
Ephesians 4:12–13

Speaking blessings over fellow believers can help accomplish this. Many Christians embrace negative attitudes about themselves, their future and others. The Word of God explains the power of possessing a dream or vision for our future because *"where there is no vision, the people perish, "* (Proverbs 29:18 KJV). When we release the power of God's life-changing Word, their lives will be transformed, their minds will be renewed (Romans 12:2).

God has given us the ministry of reconciliation and committed to us the word of reconciliation (II Corinthians 5:18–19). On many occasions, I have witnessed a positive reaction within people when I speak a blessing over them and close with, "In Jesus' Name." With a change in their countenance, they smile and say, "Thank you." Our spirits connect through our eyes. This simple exchange often provides a platform for further discussion of the Lord, His support and love for them. I am truly amazed at the power of the Spoken Blessing to touch lives for God's Kingdom.

If you hear someone expressing doubt about their abilities, their future, even, disappointments with their past, you could speak a blessing filled with Truth to combat the lies that are echoing in their mind and heart.

"May you always remember that before you were in your mother's womb, God knew you. Before you were born, God consecrated you, setting you aside for His holy purposes. He has appointed you to do great and mighty things for His kingdom. May you trust in God's Word as He declared that His plans for you are for peace and not evil, to give you a future and a hope."
Jeremiah 1:5; 29:11

In conversing with a Sunday School teacher, you might hear them express their discouragement or frustration with a situation or person (that does happen even in the best churches). Encourage them with this blessing:

"May you not lose heart in doing good, for in due time you will reap if you do not grow weary. May you be assured that God is not unjust so as to forget your work and the love you have shown toward His name, in having ministered and in still ministering to the . . . {children, adults, teens, homeless}."
Galatians 6:9; Hebrews 6:10

Someone else needs to be blessed during our worship services, at work, at home, and at play:

"I will extol Thee, my God, O King; and I will bless Thy name forever and ever. Every day I will bless Thee, And I will praise Thy name forever and ever.
Psalm 145:1–2

Every day, we should express our adoration and gratitude to our Lord.

Every day, we are to lift His name above every name, confessing His Lordship over our lives.

Every day, we will praise His works and declare His mighty acts to others.

Every day, His godly ones shall bless Him.

When I do what I just suggested, I gain strength and am renewed in my inner being to accomplish all that God has commanded me. How can I lose? How can I feel defeated when I focus on my God, who He is to me and to His world? As you bless the Lord, every day, your confidence will increase and become solidified as a foundation in your life. It is from this strong assurance in God that we feel confident in speaking His blessings on others.

Let's consider our final example of "regular events" for blessing others:

4.   Caring for a child:

Cal and I began blessing our youngest child, *before* we discovered that I was pregnant with him. {I will discuss this in Chapter 7}. Therefore, it was only natural for me to continue to bless David once he arrived. After his morning bath, I applied baby lotion to different parts of his body. As I moved from one area to another, I blessed him using the familiar "Armor of God" passage found in Ephesians 6:

> *"May you put on the Helmet of Salvation, knowing Jesus as*
> *your personal Savior."*

{As a three-year-old, David asked Jesus to come live in his heart. Two years later, in a children's service, David accepted Jesus as his Savior. As a child's understanding of Jesus develops, he may feel a need to repeat his confession of belief in Jesus.}

I continued to apply lotion as I moved across his little body:

"May you always wear the Breastplate of Righteousness.
May you love the Lord, your God, with all your heart, and with
all your soul and with all your mind."
Matthew 22:37

As I was completing this part, the Lord spoke to me, instructing me to finish that blessing. I paused, then realized what He meant. I continued with the passage in Matthew 22:39. . . .

"May you love your neighbor as yourself."

At that time, David was a few months old. I did not understand the significance of including that part, but I obeyed. I trusted that God knew David's future and the "purpose under heaven" for David's life.

Four years later, I was preparing to speak for a ladies' conference. The Lord directed me to a scripture, then opened my heart and eyes as to the reason behind David's blessing:

"A new commandment I give to you, that you love one another,
even as I have loved you, that you also love one another.
By this all men will know that your are My disciples,
if you have love for one another."
John 13: 34–35

By relating this scripture to David's blessing, the Lord allowed me to peer into David's destiny. That one glance motivated me to continue speaking blessings which encouraged David's love and compassion for others.

"David, may you be kind to others,
tender-hearted, forgiving

others, just as God in Christ has forgiven you."
Ephesians 4:32

Even if you don't fully understand the depth and magnitude of the blessing, follow the Spirit's leading.

When is the Spoken Blessing given? Anytime God's Spirit prompts you to bless, do so. His Spirit knows what a person needs and when they need it. *When* God's Spirit prompts you to bless, obey. Even if you don't fully understand the depth and magnitude of the blessing, follow the Spirit's leading. Remember, God's ways and thoughts are higher and greater than ours. We simply want to agree with His ways, causing them to prosper in our hearts, hands and mouths.

We can bless others at the appropriate time for 'nonrecurring events.' Usually, you have time to prepare a blessing for these occasions. As the Word declares: Jesus sits at the right hand of the Father, interceding on our behalf (Romans 8:34). That is, He continually prepares the way for us, anticipating our needs and desires.

You, too, can prepare blessings for various occasions, anticipating a need:

Nonrecurring Occasions to Bless Others with a Spoken Blessing

1. **High school prom or graduation.**
Many parents of teenagers become concerned for their

safety as Prom Night and Graduation approach. Most of us have read about tragedies that have occurred on those specific nights. Too many teenagers have lost their lives or their budding futures to accidents that have happened during those celebrations. We have a great opportunity to pray and bless our children before they leave on these special evenings.

On the night of our second son's prom, I was busily preparing dinner for the family. Into the kitchen strolled Peyton, looking quite handsome in his tuxedo. He made this momma proud! Do you know what he said? "Momma, will you bless me?" I wanted to cry. Even as I spoke a blessing, I struggled not to weep. This was the son I described in the Preface of this book: Sharing Shadows. This time, my tearfulness was not from anguish, but from gratitude and delight. I was grateful to God for the transformation that had occurred within Peyton. I was proud of our son for excelling and making good choices within his life.

A portion of Peyton's blessing follows:

"May you dwell in the shelter of the Most High.
May you abide in the shadow of the Almighty.
May you make the Lord your refuge.
May no evil befall you. May He give His angels
charge concerning you, to guard you in all your ways.
Because you have loved Him, may the Lord deliver
you and set you securely on high."
Psalm 91:1,10,11,14

2.   Marriage

In Chapter 1, we read Rebekah's blessing that was spoken over her by her family as she prepared to leave. We discussed how Rebekah carried this blessing into her marriage with Isaac, who also added a blessing to their union.

Think about what you would like to see happen within someone's marriage: love for the Lord, love for each other, children, peace, prosperity, provision, satisfaction, etc. Grab your Bible and turn to its Concordance. I also use *The New Strong's Exhaustive Concordance of the Bible.* Look up different topics and their references. Locate the passages and principles identified in the Word. Write them in the format: *"May the Lord . . . "* or *"May you . . ."*

The reason we use the word, "may," is that the Hebrew language has two verb tenses: past and present/future. The English language has three verb tenses: past, present, future. Our word, "May" is used to convey the Hebrew verb tense—present/future.

> *"May your focus be on the Lord as you trust in Him,*
> *and He will keep you in perfect peace.*
> *May God grant you His wisdom upon which you will*
> *build your house.*
> *May He give you understanding in all things which will become*
> *the foundation of your home.*
> *May the knowledge of Him and His ways fill your rooms*
> *with all precious and pleasant riches.*
> *May you not neglect doing good and sharing,*
> *for with such sacrifices God is pleased.*
> *May God equip you in every good thing to do His will,*
> *working in you that which is pleasing in His sight."*
> **Isaiah 26:3; Proverbs 24:3,4; Hebrews 13:16,21**

Another key issue in the timing of the Spoken Blessing is indicated in Proverbs 3:27–28:

> *"Do not withhold good from those to whom it is due,*
> *When it is in your power to do it.*
> *Do not say to your neighbor, 'Go, and come back,*
> *And tomorrow I will give it,'*
> *When you have it with you."*

"When" is then.

When someone asks you to pray for them, or to bless them, don't hesitate. Do it, then. "When" is then. Remember the definition of 'kairos' implies not the convenience of the season, but the necessity of the *task at hand* whether the time provides a good, convenient opportunity or not. Too many times I have agreed to pray for someone, then walked away and forgotten about doing it. Now, I make every effort to pray and bless them, right then! People are always grateful that I take the time to do it. God's peace enters and His Spirit directs my words. The recipient leaves filled with reassurance of God's love and purpose for them. They depart richer than they came; more determined to be victorious. I feel satisfied when God uses me.

Set Times

The final definition of 'time' is a "set time." This reminds me of a scheduled or planned event, one for which you have time to prepare a blessing.

Some of those 'set times' might be: a baby shower, bridal shower, 'going away' party, 50th birthday party, or a retirement party. Before you begin writing, ask God how He would like to bless this person. Ask Him what He desires to activate, stimulate or renew within their life. Consider the circumstances surrounding them. Meditate on the Word, reflecting on the 'time or season' of this person's life. Proverbs 25:11 explains:

"Like apples of gold in settings of silver is a
word spoken in right circumstances."

Adorn your friend with the beauty of the Lord by releasing His Word over their life.

Imagine the beauty of God's Word being gracefully draped about that person's neck as silver entwined with gold. The silver of redemption, blended with the gold of divinity, produces a magnificent picture of our Lord Jesus. The Lord's delight and purpose is for the redemption and restoration of His creation; restoring the divine image of their original being. Adorn your friend with the beauty of the Lord by releasing His Word over their life. Speak forth God's desire by releasing, through the power of the Spoken Blessing, His work within the lives of others.

May I do the same for you:

*May you always remember that God's love
for you has no beginning and no end, for
it is everlasting, forever and ever.
May you feel His strong arm supporting you and His
faithful love strengthening you. May you recognize
His favor operating within your life. May you see
His hand of provision, meeting your every need. May
you learn to trust in the timeliness of His answers.
May you draw near to Him, seeking His
understanding for your dilemmas.
May His Spirit bring to your remembrance*

the Word of Christ giving you instruction
and direction for your path of life.
May you rest in Him.
In Jesus' Name, Amen.

Journal of My Journey with the Spoken Blessing

When someone asks me to pray for them, I usually:

_____
_____
_____
_____.

I will change my reaction and response to them by:

_____
_____
_____
_____
_____.

God's purposes will prosper in my hands as I:

_____
_____
_____
_____
_____.

The scriptures that strengthen my confidence in speaking a blessing are:

_____
_____

_____

_____

_____

_____

_____ .

Write a blessing to honor the Lord.

_____

_____

_____

_____ .

Write a blessing pertaining to someone's business or career.

_____

_____

_____

_____

_____ .

*"The generous man will be prosperous, and he
who waters will himself be watered."*
Proverbs 11:25

Chapter 4

Where Must We Be, Spiritually, to Bless Others?

- ◆ Where must we be in our relationship with God?
- ◆ What must happen within our hearts and minds to enable us to bless others?
- ◆ What truths, found in the Word of God, must be grounded within our inner being?

"Forever, O LORD,
Thy word is settled in heaven,
Thy faithfulness continues throughout all generations;
Thou didst establish the earth, and it stands."
Psalm 119:89–90

In Hebrew, the word "settled" is *Natsab* which means: *to be set up, to be stationed, to station oneself, to stand; to be firm or healthy; to set, to place, to erect, to establish. It portrays various types of standing, waiting, postures. It means to be in a position of authority.*

Is God's Word *settled* as the authority in our lives? Have we erected any mind sets or predispositions which are contrary to God's Word? What attitudes and precepts must prevail to allow us the freedom to bless and not curse? I Peter 3:8–9 answers that question:

"To sum up, let all be harmonious, sympathetic,
brotherly, kindhearted, and humble in spirit;

not returning evil for evil,
or insult for insult, but giving a blessing
instead; for you were called
for the very purpose that you might inherit a blessing."

Verse 8 indicates that we ALL should be harmonious, sympathetic, etc. Is there even ONE of us who could truthfully say that we possess ALL those wonderful qualities to the fullest degree? These verses serve as a standard by which we judge ourselves. They set the goal for which we strive. What's a person to do? How do we reach that goal?

Consider the analogy described in II Timothy 2:20–22:

"Now in a large house there are not
only gold and silver vessels,
but also vessels of wood and of earthenware,
and some to honor and some to dishonor.
Therefore, if a man cleanses himself from these things,
he will be a vessel for honor, sanctified, useful to the
Master, prepared for every good work.
Now flee from youthful lusts, and pursue righteousness,
faith, love and peace, with those who call on the Lord
from a pure heart."

"A pure heart" closely describes the heart portrayed in I Peter 3:8–9. How do we develop and maintain a "pure heart?" II Timothy 2:21 answers that question:

"if a man cleanses himself from these things."

And what are *"these things?"* The preceding verses 16 and 19 of II Timothy 2, identify *"these things."*

*"But avoid worldly and empty **chatter**, for*
it will lead to further ungodliness,"

*" . . . Let everyone who names the name of
the Lord abstain from **wickedness.** "*

The King James Version of verse 16 reads:

*"But shun **profane** and **vain babblings**:
for they will increase unto
more **ungodliness.** "*

Anything that is "profane" is void of religion and piety.
When this word is applied to a person, it indicates a lack of all
affinity to God. *Affinity* refers to a close relationship, connec-
tion; a similarity in structure and nature. Thus, within a profane
person or within their speech, there is no resemblance to the
character and nature of God.

Webster's explained "chatter" as "rapid, foolish talk,"
whereas the definition of "babblings" is "foolish or meaningless talk; a continuous murmur." To add fuel to this ugly fire
of speech, Timothy used the descriptive word: "vain." Timothy
identified that this "meaningless talk" was "fruitless speaking,
devoid of any divine or spiritual character." This type of speech
offered nothing to the shaping and molding of the Christian life
and character. He related this to an increasing lack of reverence
toward God, and to disrespect for oneself and others.

How can these wicked murmurings *increase* ungodliness? In Numbers 13, it is noted that the Lord directed Moses
to send 12 spies to investigate the land of Canaan. This was the
same land God had given to Abraham for him and his descendants (Genesis 12:6–8). This was the land "flowing with milk
and honey" that God confirmed ownership to Moses in Exodus
3:6–8. Therefore, it was no surprise to Moses for God to give
him such instructions as found in Numbers 13. Spying out the
land of Canaan was simply the next step towards fulfilling God's
ordained plan for His people.

When these 12 spies returned with their report of the

land, they answered many of the questions Moses posed in verses 18–20. Their description of the inhabitants and their cities obviously disturbed the Israelites, for Caleb "quieted the people before Moses" (Numbers 13:30). As an expression of his faith in God and in an attempt to reassure the congregation, Caleb said, *"We should by all means go up and take possession of it, for we shall surely overcome it."* Faith in God, that was resident within him, rose up and was released by Caleb's confession.

But somewhere along the way, ten spies had forsaken their confidence in God, had forgotten ALL that God had done for them in Egypt and in their exodus. Those ten spies walked about Canaan and discarded God's word which declared that land to be His promise to them; His inheritance for them. As those ten, tribal leaders surveyed the land, inquired about the people and investigated the cities; they chose to embrace an attitude of fear, doubt and unbelief. *Canaan* is a symbol of inheritance gained by warfare. The number *40* is symbolic of probation and testing, which ends in victory or defeat. Ten spies were defeated in their faith, two spies were victorious.

Do we choose to live in victory or defeat?

Can we not learn from their mistakes? Consider the areas that tested the spies' faith: land, people and cities. What is our attitude about the geographical location in which we live? Do we call it blessed or cursed? How do we view the people we live around, work with, attend church with and recreate with? How do we interact with them? Do we notice the bad and fail to recognize the good within others? Is your city being blessed by your words; do you support the officials or condemn them? *"By the blessing of the upright a city is exalted, but by the mouth of the wicked it is torn down" (Proverbs 11:11).* Do we choose to live in victory or defeat?

Consider what happened as a result of the defeated attitudes of the ten spies.

> *"So they brought the Israelites an **evil** report of the land which they had scouted out . . ."*
> **Numbers 13:32 KJV**

"Evil" means *"bad, inferior quality; wicked; a moral deficiency; inability to come up to good standards which will benefit. It is immoral activity against other people, whether by speech, by practice or by offering improper sacrifices. This depicts a very negative inner attitude toward God or man."*

Their *wicked murmurings increased* and spread throughout the masses:

> *"Then all the congregation lifted up their voices and cried, and the people wept that night. And all the sons of Israel grumbled against Moses and Aaron; and the whole congregation said to them, 'Would that we had died in the land of Egypt! Or would that we had died in this wilderness!'"*
> **Numbers 14:1–2**

The evil, faithless words of 10 men infected thousands of people. Their profane words increased ungodliness within others to the point that a great judgment was wielded against them and the murmuring congregation.

> *"And the LORD spoke to Moses and Aaron, saying, 'How long shall I bear with this evil congregation who are grumbling against Me? I have heard the complaints of the sons of Israel, which they are making against Me.*

Say to them, "As I live," says the LORD, "just as you have
spoken in My hearing, so I will surely do to you;
your corpses shall fall in this wilderness,
even all your numbered men, according to your
complete number from twenty years old and upward,
who have grumbled against Me."
Numbers 14:26–29

"As for the men whom Moses sent to spy out the land and who
returned and made all the congregation grumble against him
by bringing out a bad report concerning the land,
even those men who brought out the very bad report
of the land died by a plague before the LORD."
Numbers 14:36–37

Where is our faith and confidence in God?

As I read that account of God's judgment, I was motivated to rethink my grumbling attitude. How about you? How
much do we complain; moaning and groaning about this incon-
venience or that difficulty? Do we perceive those "pebbles" in
the road as though they were "towering mountains?" Where is
our faith and confidence in God?

Josephus, a Jewish historian, described those 10 spies
as having elevated *their* words and perception about the land
of Canaan ABOVE the word of God. They chose to place
more value on their interpretation of the "promised land" than
on God's view. They failed to remember that God's ways and
thoughts were higher than theirs. His Word was not settled as the
authority in their lives.

Stop right here. Josephus' interpretation of those 10
spies' response pierced through me like a spear. I began to won-

der when I had ever placed my words higher than the word of the Lord. In II Corinthians 13:5, Paul instructed us to:

> *"Test yourselves to see if you are in the*
> *faith; examine yourselves!"*

Personally speaking, I was moved to repentance. Have you ever made statements like: "You just wait and see. That store won't last a year;" or "You are such a scatterbrain. Why can't you remember what I told you," or "Why should I try? I'll just fail. I can't do it," or "Oh, forgive me, it's my memory, it's so bad." Give God's Holy Spirit the freedom to convict you of sin and exhort you to a life of righteousness: a right relationship with God, a recognition of the authority of His Word and submission to His Spirit.

> *"If we say that we have no sin, we are deceiving ourselves,*
> *and the truth is not in us.*
> *If we confess our sins, He is faithful and righteous to forgive*
> *us our sins and to cleanse us from all unrighteousness."*
> *I John 1:8–9*

Allow this sobering word to remain with you for a long time. It will serve as a reminder to humble your words and thoughts to those of our Almighty God.

Life Application:

Every believer has God's Promised Land, waiting for them to enter. Remember that *Canaan* represented one's inheritance gained through warfare. Consider this:

"For though we walk in the flesh, we do
not war according to the flesh,
for the weapons of our warfare are not of the flesh, but
divinely powerful for the destruction of fortresses.
We are destroying speculations and every lofty thing raised up
against the knowledge of God, and we are taking every
thought captive to the obedience of Christ,"
II Corinthians 10:3–5

We should not settle for anything less than God's best in our lives. We should embrace His Truth rather than the defeating words of others or ourselves. Those destructive words and perceptions could cause us to "wander in the wilderness" instead of stepping into our inheritance, God's Promised Land. *Wilderness wanderings* represent failure and unbelief to enter one's inheritance. When you are told: "Oh, that will never happen" or "that's impossible," even, "there is no way for you to get that," don't accept it as true. Ask God what He thinks. Ask Him what His word declares about your hopes and dreams.

"For I know the plans I have for you," declares the LORD,
"plans for welfare and not for calamity to
give you a future and a hope."
Jeremiah 29:11

"a week, in the mountains, with snow."

Life Application:

My family and I have been vacationing around the country for almost twenty years. We have used a timeshare exchange company to assist us. A few years ago, our 4-year-old David announced that he wanted to go to the mountains for a week; wanting to see snow. We live in Florida, so SNOW was a big deal to him. David and I began to pray every night for: "a week, in the mountains, with snow."

Earlier that year, we had visited Blowing Rock, NC, and loved it! So, we requested the same location for a week during Christmas. Our timeshare company offered no encouraging words; just the opposite: "there is no way you can get into that resort again, especially during Christmas." David and I continued to call upon God; to call it forth (Numbers 6:27). By the first week of December, we had not heard from our exchange company. Several phone calls later, coupled with God's grace, we were given a week, during Christmas, in Blowing Rock. As we drove up the mountain, we could not see snow, but, that meant the roads were clear and hazard-free. We continued to walk by faith and not by sight. We anticipated snow on Christmas Day. Much to our delight, HUGE snowflakes began to fall on Christmas morning! We caught it on camera. Blowing Rock became a "winter wonderland." What a 'faith builder' that was for David, and for me. God gave us the desires of our heart. He does not disappoint. Even now, I remind David of that time when we prayed for snow. It serves as a memorial to the faithfulness of God to answer our prayers and to respond to our faith.

Examine *where* your faith is. Don't miss out on all the promises of God by listening to and accepting defeating words and circumstances. Bless yourself and others with the truth of God's Word.

"Take care, brethren, lest there should
be in any one of you an evil,
unbelieving heart, in falling away from the living God.
But encourage one another day after day, as long as it is still
called 'Today,' lest any one of you be hardened by the
deceitfulness of sin.

> *For we have become partakers of Christ, if we hold fast*
> *the beginning of our assurance firm until the end."*
> **Hebrews 3:12–14**

By speaking the Word of Truth as we release blessings into people's lives, we are warring against the spirits of deception, theft and destruction. We recognize the enemy as one who comes to steal, kill and destroy (John 10:10). We must hold fast to our confession, knowing that faith is required to enter God's promise (Hebrews 4:14; 11:6).

We can hear this message, but if it is not united by faith, it will not profit us (Hebrews 4:2). When we hear the word of God's message and accept it for what it really is, the Word of God, then the word performs its work in us who believe (I Thessalonians 2:13). We are instructed to bless, which will pave the way for our inheriting our blessing, our land of milk and honey (I Peter 3:9).

Consider what our lips can do for others:

> *"The tongue of the righteous is as choice silver, . . ."*
> *"The lips of the righteous feed many, . . ."*
> *"The lips of the righteous bring forth what is acceptable, . . ."*
> **Proverbs 10:20, 21, 32**

Proverbs 10 identifies the positive potential of our mouths. James 3:5–12 exposes the opposite: the power of a sinful tongue. With our tongue, we can bless our Lord, but with it we curse men, who have been created in His image. If James 3 describes you, then, consider the cause.

> *"But the things that proceed out of the*
> *mouth come from the heart,*
> *and those defile the man."*
> **Matthew 15:18**

When we love God with all our heart, there is no 'throne-room' left for our pain and offense. How do you cleanse your heart of bad attitudes, doubt, fear and unbelief?

Step 1: **Forgive those who have hurt you.** Ask God's Spirit to show you who you need to forgive. It is a choice you must make. It is a form of worship. When we love God with all our heart, there is no 'throne-room' left for our pain and offense. Many have made idols out of their offenses. Forgive others, just as Christ has forgiven you (Ephesians 4:32).

The *Tallahassee Democrat* published an article by Julie Sevrens, entitled: "Forgiveness can heal." She identified that "scientists have launched research that has begun to demonstrate that forgiveness can positively enhance emotional and, quite possibly, physical health." Ms. Sevrens cited a study that linked anger with an increased risk of heart attacks and identified its negative influences on the body's immune system. Also noted was research which had found "that the less people forgave, the more diseases they had, and the more medical symptoms they reported." "You can actually change a person's well-being, their emotions, by helping them to forgive," stated Robert Enright, professor of educational psychology at the University of Wisconsin (*Tallahassee Democrat,* August 2, 1999).

Step 2: **Ask forgiveness from those you have hurt**. Ask God to forgive you for causing others pain. Hebrews 12:14 clearly instructs us on this matter:

> *"Pursue peace with all men, and the*
> *sanctification without which*

no one will see the Lord."

Psalm 34:13–14 admonishes us:

"Keep your tongue from evil,
And your lips from speaking deceit.
Depart from evil, and do good;
Seek peace, and pursue it."

Step 3: Speak DEATH to the fruitless words you have spoken over your life and the lives of others.

Freeda Bowers' *Give Me 40 Days* clearly explained and encouraged this step. It reminded me of my personal experience with the power of a 'word curse' or sowing a bad seed within my life. I 'sowed' that evil seed when I was in my early 20's.

Someone spoke cruel and offensive words to me concerning my appearance. My response to my pain was to speak a malediction over myself: I vowed that I would never give birth to a daughter. But, when our two boys were of preschool age, Cal and I were ready to ask God for a third child. Having two boys, I wanted a girl. As I prayed, God reminded me of my word curse; the evil seed I had sown. I was heartbroken. Could this mean that I would never have a daughter? I cried before the Lord with a broken and contrite heart, "Forgive me, Father, I didn't know what I was doing." God did not despise my repentance. In 1986, our beautiful princess, Elizabeth Ann, was born.

"Death and life are in the power of the tongue,
And those who love it will eat its fruit."
Proverbs 18:21

Step 4: Speak LIFE over yourself and others, agreeing with the living word of God, trusting in the life-changing power of His Holy Spirit who lives within you.

"May you have faith like Abraham, as he believed that
God would give him a child. May you call
forth life over the barrenness
of your body. May you agree with God's spoken word as He
declared, 'Be fruitful and multiply.'
May you call into being those children who do not yet exist,
knowing that their spirits are in the presence of the Lord.
May you have confidence that God knows each of your children
before He places them within your womb."
In Jesus' Name, Amen.
Romans 4:17; Genesis 1:28; Jeremiah 1:5

This is one of many types of blessings which speak LIFE over someone. By faith, we can bless ourselves and others:

"By faith Isaac blessed Jacob and Esau,
even regarding things to come.
By faith Jacob, as he was dying, blessed
each of the sons of Joseph,
and worshiped, . . ."
Hebrews 11:20,21

As I referenced verse 21, I discovered Genesis 48:1–2 in which was described Israel's ailing condition: " . . . your father is sick. . . . .Israel collected his strength and sat up in bed." The meaning of "collected his strength" is "to make firm, to support, to prove courageous, valiant." Often, it referred to a battle scene. Just think about that: a battle scene. There are and will be occasions in which we will experience a battle: to bless or to curse; to release a word of confidence in the power of God working within someone's life or to pronounce a condemning expectation of their personal abilities or inabilities. The battle is within. Jacob had to rely upon his inner strength because his physical body was weak and frail. We will have to do the same. Upon whose strength can we depend? The indwelling of the Spirit of

Christ provides us with the support and resolve to speak LIFE, not death, over others. Our spoken blessings will produce a lasting effect within the lives of others because our words carry the power of our eternal God.

Releasing a blessing over others provides an atmosphere of worship and a posture of reverence.

As our blessing focuses on God's faithful loving-kindness, the trustworthiness of His character, the abundance of His provision and the never-failing forgiveness of the Cross, our hearts will move into awe and wonder of Him. Jacob moved from blessing his grandsons into worship of His God. We will do likewise.

Step 5: Gain a new mind set; a new heart attitude by washing your mind and heart with the water of God's Word.

Many children grow up under, and I mean, UNDER, the weight of a nickname. Parents begin calling a toddler some name, thinking it's cute or catchy: "Trouble," "Fireball," "Two-ton," "Klutzy," "Daredevil," etc. Some parents make excuses for a 'tendency' within their child and verbalize it in the hearing of that child: "Oh, he's just a shy one," "Oh, I know he has a temper. It's that red hair, you know," "She doesn't like to read. I don't know what I'm gonna do with her!" Older children may bear such names as: "Computer Nerd," "Couch Potato," or "Geek." These nicknames may have different connotations within various groups of people, but rarely do they have an affirming or positive meaning.

Unfortunately, many children develop the characteristic their parents emphasized by their nickname. If a person hears something often enough, they are likely to believe and embrace it. If a child gains attention for their 'tendency,' they will work to maintain it to provide MORE attention for themselves.

"For as he thinks within himself, so he is."
Proverbs 23:7

Encouragement replaces condemnation.

Reading the Word, speaking it and believing the Truth that it gives, will help remove the old ways of thinking about yourself and others. Truth replaces lies. Encouragement replaces condemnation. Bondage is destroyed, freedom is gained.

One historical figure who knew God's Word and who possessed a pure heart was Boaz. He chose to walk out his life in *faith, commitment* and *expectancy.* In Chapter 3, we discussed Boaz's blessing his workers who were reaping barley:

> *"May the LORD be with you."*
> *His reapers responded:*
> *"May the LORD bless you."*
> ***Ruth 2:4***

For Boaz to speak such a blessing indicated that he had confidence and *faith* in God's desire to be present within his life and in the lives of his workers. He was familiar enough with the Scriptures to *expect* God's blessing upon him, his employees and his fields. Boaz had a *commitment* to God's original plan and purpose of increase and multiplication. Timothy's analogy of a vessel of honor could be used to describe Boaz as one who was *"useful to the Master, prepared for every good work,"* (II Timothy 2:21).

What was the "good work" that I Peter 3:8–9 made reference to: blessing others, then, receiving our inherited blessing. Boaz not only knew "where" he needed to be, spiritually, he knew "where" God's blessings would flow. He had gained confidence in His God, by knowing His word:

> *"Blessed shall you be in the city,*

and blessed shall you be in the country (field)."
"Blessed shall be the . . . produce of your ground . . ."
"Blessed shall be your basket and your kneading bowl."
"Blessed shall you be when you come in, and
blessed shall you be when you go out."
"The LORD will command the blessing upon you
in your barns and in all that you put your hand to,
and He will bless you in the land which the LORD
your God gives you."
Deuteronomy 28:1–8

In Ruth 2:22–23, a wise Naomi recognized "where" their blessing was and instructed Ruth:

"And Naomi said to Ruth her daughter-in-law,
'It is good, my daughter, that you go out with his maids,
lest others fall upon you in another field.'
So she stayed close by the maids of Boaz in order to glean
until the end of the barley harvest and the wheat harvest.
And she lived with her mother-in-law."

Ruth submitted to and obeyed the instruction of Naomi. *Barley* is a symbol of poverty, lowliness and low reputation. Jesus taught in Matthew 5:3: *"Blessed are the poor in spirit, for theirs is the kingdom of heaven."* We must recognize our impoverished, spiritual emptiness allowing room for the King of Glory to enter our lives. Ruth had nothing, and she knew it. Her inheritance was linked to Naomi and to Boaz. She was no fool. Ruth understood the importance of staying close to her blessing. Take note that she stayed and gleaned through the wheat harvest. *Wheat* represents the staff of life, the bread of Christ and of His saints. Jesus identified that the person with a humbled spirit, within which He is given control, is rewarded with His presence: the kingdom of heaven. Within His kingdom, all blessings flow.

Where are you spiritually?

1. **Become confident in God's desire and eagerness to develop His divine nature within people.**

God knows us as spiritual beings and gives us a physical body while we live on the earth. Therefore, He knew us before He placed us within our mother's womb (Jeremiah 1:5). Just as God had a plan for Jeremiah's life, He has a purpose for you and me. As Jeremiah was to be consecrated and appointed as God's prophet, his character needed to reflect submission to God. Knowing that we all deal with sin, we need the redemptive power of Christ working within us, replacing our old ways with His new ways (II Corinthians 5:17). The working of His divine nature within us never ceases. God continually thinks about us: our past, our present and our future (Jeremiah 29:11). As God consecrated Jeremiah, He sets us apart from the world, to become pure and devoted to Him. This is the message of Timothy's analogy of the vessels used for honor and dishonor (II Timothy 2:20). In Psalm 139, David gave tribute to His Creator for his life:

"For Thou didst form my inward parts;
Thou didst weave me in my mother's womb.
I will give thanks to Thee, for I am fearfully and
wonderfully made; wonderful are Thy works, and
my soul knows it very well. My frame was not
hidden from Thee, when I was made in secret,
and skillfully wrought in the depths of the earth.
Thine eyes have seen my unformed substance;
and in Thy book there were all written,
the days that were ordained for me,
when as yet there was not one of them."
Psalm 139:13–16

Become confident that the Lord values each person and His image that is being developed within that person.

2.   Choose to trust God to accomplish His divine plan for yourself and for others.

> *"For it is God who is at work in you,*
> *both to **will** and to **work** for His good pleasure."*
> **Philippians 2:13**

The Greek word for *will* is *Thelo* which means: not only to will something, but also pressing into action. It refers to seeing one's desire to its execution: *"there is . . . a time for every purpose under the heaven." Energeo* is the Greek word for *work*. It refers to being active and energetic, effective, proving oneself to be strong.

Allow me to use these definitions to add depth to verse 13:

> *"for it is God who is actively working in you;*
> *pressing into action and energetically,*
> *effectively proving Himself strong in*
> *accomplishing His good desire and pleasure."*

Definitions of words add richness and volume to our understanding of the message. Within us, we house thousands of definitions and concepts of words which may be accurate or erroneous. An example of this, is the word, *perfect.* Many people try to excuse their shortcomings by commenting: "Well, nobody's perfect." In saying this, the person admits to his flaws, trying to excuse his inability or his *unwillingness to sacrifice* to reach a higher standard. Thankfully, we serve and love a God Who is strong when we are weak.

> *"For I am confident of this very thing,*
> *that He who began a good work in you*
> *will **perfect** it until the day of Christ Jesus."*
> **Philippians 1:6**

In other words, God will finish, complete and accomplish what He started. He is not a quitter. He is our beginning and our end.

> *"Therefore you are to be **perfect,** as your*
> *heavenly Father is perfect."*
> **Matthew 5:48**

> *"And let endurance have its perfect*
> *result, that you may be **perfect***
> *and complete, lacking in nothing."*
> **James 1:4**

The Greek word being used in the latter two passages refers to *completed growth.* Yet, it is not a static state. This level of perfection describes one who has attained his moral end, the goal for which he was intended: to be obedient in Christ. Having reached this level, new opportunities will be opened before him to have Christ formed in him more and more.

> *"And all of us, as with unveiled face,*
> *[because we] continued to behold*
> *[in the Word of God] as in a mirror the glory of the Lord,*
> *are constantly being transfigured into His very own image*
> *in ever increasing splendor and from one degree of glory*
> *to another; [for this comes] from the Lord [Who is] the Spirit."*
> **II Corinthians 3:18 AMP**

Thus, we understand the magnitude of God's work within us and others. It gives Him great delight and pleasure to accomplish His plan in our lives. As proud parents, Cal and I have watched several of our children walk down the aisles of their high school and college graduations; tassels swinging, faces beaming and hands waving with "Pomp and Circumstance" playing loudly. We have experienced the continual, energetic work that a parent contributes to a child's education and training. As parents, we have had to prove ourselves strong on behalf of our children's sake. Besides the Lord, parents should be their child's strongest advocate, defending them and correcting them, helping them to achieve their destiny in God's Kingdom. Yet, we are just a shadow of the *perfect* work that God delights in accomplishing within His children.

3. **Approach your relationship with God and your life with**: *expectancy, faith* and *commitment.*

As we discussed in Chapter 1, these three components were obvious in the parents of the children who were brought to Jesus. Review their story in Mark 10:13–16:

> *"And they were bringing children to Him*
> *so that He might touch them;*
> *and the disciples rebuked them.*
> *But when Jesus saw this, He was indignant and said to them,*
> *'Permit the children to come to Me; do not hinder them;*
> *for the kingdom of God belongs to such as these.*
> *Truly I say to you, whoever does not*
> *receive the kingdom of God*
> *like a child shall not enter it at all.'*
> *And He took them in His arms and began blessing them,*
> *laying His hands upon them."*

The blessing of the Lord sets us apart . . .

Notice the perseverance of the parents. They did not allow the disciples to stop them from reaching Jesus. We should always seek after God; always desiring to be in His presence. Our firsthand, personal experience with Jesus should be so fulfilling that we are motivated to be with Him. The parents in this passage had either heard about or had had firsthand experience with the power and authority of Christ. They had *expectations* and *faith* in Jesus to do something good for their children. We are no different. We want our children to reap benefits. How many of us, parents, have stood in a long line to purchase something that our child really wanted? We have believed that the special toy or game would satisfy a longing in their heart. A parent wants their child's needs and wants to be met. The parents in Mark 10 were *committed* to the *task at hand. "To everything there is a season, and a time to every purpose under the heaven"* (Ecclesiastes 3:1). They wanted the blessing of the Lord to rest upon their children. Should we desire any less for our children and for others? When Jesus took their children into His strong arms, He blessed them; consecrating them for divine use. He set them apart from the mundane and profane things of this world. The blessing of the Lord sets us apart, sets our future apart, sets our eternal destiny apart for His glory and for the multiplication of His Kingdom. In a similar fashion, Jesus blessed the five loaves and two fish. The food was miraculously multiplied for the feeding of thousands and for bringing glory to His heavenly Father (Mark 6:41). When we bless others, miraculous events occur: needs are met, lives are restored, hope is encouraged, truth is imparted, all to the glory of God.

The children's parents knew WHERE they could find their blessing. Where is your blessing? Under whose authority, under whose covering should you submit?

WHERE can you give blessings to others?

Ask God to provide you with divine appointments every day. Ask Him to help you identify them and to be in tune with His Spirit, so that you may give a blessing in the proper season and at the right time.

Life Application:

One Saturday evening, I ran into a store to purchase something. As I was checking out, the clerk sighed deeply, expressing how tired she was. Despondently she mentioned her being scheduled to work on Sunday, not being able to attend her church service. I encouraged her to invite Jesus to work with her the next day. Then, I spoke a blessing of God's rest and restoration over her. The clerk's countenance changed. She became more cheerful and relaxed.

WHERE must we be, spiritually, to bless others? How should our "horizontal" {⟷} relationships appear?
1. harmonious
2. sympathetic
3. brotherly
4. kind-hearted
5. humble in spirit
   We must love our neighbor as ourselves
   (Matthew 22:39).

What must happen within our hearts and minds to enable us to bless?
1. cleanse ourselves from worldly and
   empty chatter and from wickedness
2. forgive others and seek forgiveness from others
3. speak death to bad words and attitudes
4. speak life, agreeing with God's Word of Faith

What truths found in the Word of God must be grounded within our being?
1. God desires for us to become vessels of honor:
   our speech should feed many and speak forth what is
   acceptable.

2.   God desires to bless us and others.
3.   God has a purpose for every person.
4.   God is trustworthy and will accomplish His will
             and His work.

Where must we be in our "vertical" { ↕ } relationship with God?
      His Spirit of Truth must have complete authority in our heart, soul and mind. When combined, our "horizontal" and "vertical" relationships portray the Cross {✝}, through which our inherited blessing originates and emanates.

What mind sets and conditions of our hearts must prevail to allow us the freedom to bless and curse not?
1.   We should be full of faith in Jesus.
2.   We should have expectancy in our hearts.
3.   We should be committed to His goals and purposes.

His goal is for you to walk in His blessing:

"May the Lord cause you to prosper
and excel in all that you do.
May all that you do be done to the glory of God.
May others see your good work and
offer praise to Him and Him alone.
May you be perfected in your obedience to Him.
May you be reassured that He loves you and
takes great delight in spending time with you.
May you reserve special sessions of
"one-on-one" time with the Lord.
May He share with you His special intimacies,
preserved for His righteous ones.

May you offer a sacrifice of praise and thanksgiving for the wonderful gift of His love. In Jesus' Name, Amen.

Journal of My Journey with the Spoken Blessing

At this time, I would describe my relationship with God as:

_____

_____

_____

_____

_____

_____ .

I will improve it by:

_____

_____

_____

_____ .

I will forgive:

_____

_____

_____

_____

_____ .

I will ask forgiveness for:

_____

_____

_____

_____

_____.

I will improve my relationships with others by:

_____

_____

_____

_____.

Write a blessing for a family member or friend.

_____

_____

_____

_____

_____

_____.

"He who loves purity of heart and whose speech
is gracious, the king is his friend."
Proverbs 22:11

Chapter 5

Why Should We Use the Spoken Blessing?

"Then the LORD spoke to Moses, saying,
'Speak to Aaron and to his sons, saying,
"Thus you shall bless the sons of Israel. You shall say to them:
The LORD bless you, and keep you;
the LORD make His face shine on you,
and be gracious to you;
the LORD lift up His countenance on you,
and give you peace."
So they shall invoke My name on the sons of Israel,
and I then will bless them.'"
Numbers 6:22–27

To "invoke" means to bless, to call for a blessing, to put into use or to call forth. The King James translation reads: *"And they shall **put My name upon** the children of Israel, and I will bless them."*

God's name reflects His character, His person. Is there anything more powerful than His name? We are 'to put to use' and 'call forth' His name. Who is like the Lord? Is there anything more perfect than His divine name, His holy nature?

Recall that God has shown Himself to be committed to:

1. His **creation**
2. His **covenant**
3. His **name and character**.

WHO was instructed to "invoke" or "put God's name upon" the people?

Aaron and his sons were given the command. Who were they? Aaron and his sons had been appointed and anointed to be the Lord's priests. God gave them and their positions certain authority, responsibilities and privileges. These priests understood the gravity and consequences of their office.

As Aaron and his sons were the priests within the Old Covenant, who are their counterparts within the New Covenant; in this present dispensation of Christ's Church?

"you also, as living stones, are being
built up as a spiritual house
for a holy priesthood, to offer up spiritual
sacrifices acceptable to
God through Jesus Christ.
But you are a CHOSEN RACE, A ROYAL PRIESTHOOD,
A HOLY NATION, A PEOPLE FOR
GOD'S OWN POSSESSION,
that you may proclaim the excellencies of Him who has called
you out of darkness into His marvelous light;"
I Peter 2:5,9

"But you will be called the priests of the LORD;
you will be spoken of as ministers of our God.
You will eat the wealth of nations,
and in their riches you will boast."
Isaiah 61:6

You and I, believers in the Lord Jesus Christ, are His priests. As we serve as priests to God, we execute His instruction and command to bless.

WHY should we use the Spoken Blessing? We are to proclaim the excellencies of our Lord *and* we are commanded to do so.

Recall I Peter 3:9:

> " . . . but giving a blessing instead; for
> you were called for the very
> purpose that you might inherit a blessing."

In Greek, the word *called* is *kaleo* which means to invite; of the divine invitation to participate in the blessings of redemption; to be called by name. It suggests either vocation or destination.

We are to look for and anticipate God providing opportunities for us to bless others.

As we serve God as priests and ministers, we are to fulfill His will and His commitment to BLESS. As we bless, we receive blessings as Galatians 6:7–10 identifies:

> *"Do not be deceived, God is not mocked;
> for whatever a man sows,
> this he will also reap.
> For the one who sows to his own flesh shall from the flesh
> reap corruption, but the one who sows
> to the Spirit shall from the
> Spirit reap eternal life.
> And let us not lose heart in doing good,
> for in due time we shall reap if we do not grow weary.
> So then, while we have opportunity,
> let us do good to all men,
> and especially to those who are of the household of the faith."*

We are to look for and anticipate God providing opportunities for us to bless others.

Ask Him what you can do each day that would bring Him glory and honor. Anticipation of God going before us creates an excitement and a joy that is visible upon our countenance, heard within our words and witnessed in the spiritual realm.

> *"You are the light of the world. A city*
> *set on a hill cannot be hidden.*
> *Nor do men light a lamp, and put it*
> *under the peck-measure, but on*
> *the lampstand; and it gives light to all who are in the house.*
> *Let your light shine before men in such a way that they may*
> *see your good works, and glorify your*
> *Father who is in heaven."*
> **Matthew 5:14–16**

. . . obedience in this area has a direct consequence: inheriting our blessing . . .

Remember, we are being built up (and we are building up others) as a spiritual house through which we offer to God spiritual sacrifices. We give His light to those who are in our dwelling or work place: within our sphere of influence. Each of us has a realm in which we work, live, serve and recreate. What impact are we having in these areas? Do others know that we are a believer in the Lord Jesus?

Within these different spheres, throughout our 'walks of life,' we will experience offenses, maledictions, biases and misunderstandings. Our command is to bless and to not return the curse. How many of us can attest to the 'sacrifice of our flesh' when we DO NOT retaliate with harsh words or criticism? How many of us have poured 'cool' words on the top of 'hot heads?' We must continue to strongly encourage and help each other achieve this level of humility and submission to His command because obedience in this area has a direct consequence: inheriting our blessing (I Peter 3:9). Not returning evil for evil, but giving a blessing instead, is an 'over-comers outlook.' Over-comers receive their inheritance (Revelation 21:7).

Consider a biblical character who satisfied his physical desires or served his 'flesh,' disregarding the value of his spiritual inheritance:

> *"See to it that no one comes short of the grace of God;*
> *that no root of bitterness springing up causes trouble,*
> *and by it many be defiled;*
> *that there be no immoral or godless person like Esau,*
> *who sold his own birthright for a single meal.*
> *For you know that even afterwards, when he desired to inherit*
> *a blessing, he was rejected, for he found*
> *no place for repentance,*
> *though he sought for it with tears."*
> ***Hebrews 12: 15–17***

Life Application:

When someone offends us, we have a choice to make: to bless or to curse them. A blessing operates within the spiritual realm of ourselves and the offender. A curse patronizes the fleshly, carnal level of both people. *We must decide into which realm we will sow; for, from that realm, we will reap.* If we place more value in retaliation and protecting our image, reputation or 'rights,' then, we place less value on our future spiritual inheritance. There will be no repentance found within our hearts. That is to say, we will continue throughout life with a bitter, unchanged heart. We will lose the promised blessing, though we seek it with tears.

A side note: Esau loved his 'flesh' and wanted to have immediate gratification instead of sacrificing and patiently waiting for his promised inheritance and blessing. Let this be a warning to us! Spend time with this Life Application. Meditate on it until God's Spirit completes His instruction for you. Allow Him to personalize this lesson.

Chuck D. Pierce, a man who is consecrated to serving as a mighty intercessor of God, sent a word from the Lord directing us to "Seven Days of Stillness: A Prayer Focus to Renew Your Spirit." Within this directive, the Lord instructed us to be still and allow Him to quiet and purify our hearts. Our sin had to be dealt a fatal blow. Our hearts had to be purified. The message that pierced my heart was that I had to eliminate all "dangerous emotions" that would cause me to miss the fullness of my eternal destiny. The word of the Lord said:

"My people are filled with dangerous emotions. I want to settle their emotions so that their mind will think the same way that I think. Unless they allow Me to deal with their dangerous emotions they will miss many blessings that I have for the future. Many will end up striking the rock as Moses did out of a dangerous emotion instead of speaking to the rock and miss their door of entry for this season. Tell My people to be still."
"I am calling for a Jericho stillness. This warfare call is important for the future of My people. If they will come before Me for seven

straight days and allow Me to still their
hearts and quiet their spirits,
that which has been invincible in their past and has kept them
from moving into their future will fall before them.
Tell MY people to still their hearts before Me. "

I observed this Stillness Fast. God was faithful to show me what I had to accomplish, every day, to overcome my dangerous emotion. Esau's love of self was more important to him than his inheritance in God (Genesis 25:29–34). Moses' self-love overshadowed his love for the Lord and His Promised Land (Numbers 20:1–13). I do not want to love myself, my emotions, my rights or reputation more than I love God and His eternity.

May you reach the point in your life where you can declare as Paul did in Acts 20:24, 27:

"But I do not consider my life of any account as dear to myself,
in order that I may finish my course, and the ministry which
I received from the Lord Jesus, to testify solemnly of the gospel
of the grace of God. "
"For I did not shrink from declaring to
you the whole purpose of God. "

May you follow Paul's example found in Acts 20:32, 35:

"And now I commend you to God and to the word of His grace,
which is able to build you up and to give you the inheritance
among all those who are sanctified. "
"In everything I showed you that by
working hard in this manner you
must help the weak and remember the words of the Lord Jesus,
that He Himself said, 'It is more blessed
to give than to receive.'"

Makarios is the Greek word used in verse 35, which

is translated as *blessed*. It indicates the state of the believer in Christ. The believer is indwelt by God because of Christ and as a result is fully satisfied. A *blessed* person is one whom God makes fully satisfied, not because of favorable circumstances, but because He indwells the believer through Christ. To be *makarios,* "blessed," is equivalent to having God's kingdom within one's heart. Submission to the control and authority of God's Holy Spirit allows us to experience "the kingdom of God" in our lives.

When we bless others, we speak well of them, we consecrate them for divine use, we call forth God's name and character to be formed within them through the presence and power of His Spirit. As we speak a blessing over someone's life, we build them up, encouraging them to operate in the spiritual realm and to focus on their destiny within God's Kingdom. An end result of speaking blessings is to assist others in turning away from their iniquities (Acts 3:26).

As Paul recognized the ministry which he had been given (Acts 20:24), you and I have been given the ministry of reconciliation as stated in II Corinthians 5:18–20:

"Now all these things are from God, who
reconciled us to Himself through Christ,
and gave us the ministry of reconciliation,
namely, that God was in Christ reconciling
the world to Himself,
not counting their trespasses against them,
and He has committed to us the word of reconciliation.
Therefore, we are ambassadors for Christ, as though God
were entreating through us; we beg you on behalf of Christ,
be reconciled to God."

God so deeply longed for His people to be "one with Him" that Jesus humbled Himself to suffer death on a cross, before the foundations of the earth had been laid (Rev. 13:8). God is All-knowing. He knew what it would take for His creation to be restored and redeemed from sin. God desired for His creation to be reconciled to Him and restored to his original position of *authority,* his original covering of *glory* (i.e.: His substantive presence), his original *fellowship* with Him. God gave Adam and Eve **authority**:

"And God blessed them and said to them, Be fruitful, multiply, and fill the earth, and subdue it [using all its vast resources in the service of God and man]; and have dominion over the fish of the sea, the birds of the air, and over every living creature that moves upon the earth."
Genesis 1:28 AMP

Originally, God's spiritual image was the composition of Adam and Eve:

"Then God said, 'Let Us make man in Our image, according to Our likeness; . . . '"
Genesis 1:26

"And the man and his wife were both naked and were not embarrassed or ashamed in each other's presence."
Genesis 2:25 AMP

We also read about this manifestation of God's **glory** in Exodus 34:29. Moses' face glowed as a result of being in the presence of God. That external manifestation faded (II Corinthians 3:7). But the ministry of the Spirit transforms us from glory to glory, restoring within us the original image of God, His nature and character (II Corinthians 3:18).

Adam and Eve, originally, experienced intimate **fellowship** with God as is implied in Genesis 3:8,9:

"And they heard the sound of the LORD
God walking in the garden
in the cool of the day, and the man and his wife hid
themselves from the presence of the LORD God
among the trees of the garden.
Then the LORD God called to the man, and said to him,
'Where are you?'"

As ministers of reconciliation, we can bless others with God's Word of Truth, building them up in their faith, encouraging restoration of their authority, God's glory, and fellowship with Him (II Corinthians 10:8). We can declare with confidence:

"May God cause you to prosper and excel
in all that you do as He did
Joseph. May others elevate you into positions of authority
as they regard God's favor upon you. May others be
blessed through your relationship with the Lord."
Genesis 39:2–6

May the Lord be your glory and the One who lifts your head.
May you trust in God to complete and perfect the good work
He has begun in you. May you be trained in His righteousness,
moving from glory to glory. May you be conformed to the
image of His Son, Who is full of glory."
Psalm 3:3; Philippians 1:6; Romans 8:29; 9:23

"May God make known to you the path of life.
May you discover that in His presence is fullness of joy;
in His right hand there are pleasures forever.
May you know Christ, the power of His resurrection
and the fellowship of His sufferings, being conformed
to His death in order to attain to the resurrection
from the dead. May you enter into eternal
fellowship with your Lord.
Psalm 16:11; Philippians 3:10–11

As fellow believers we can exhibit similar support as Aaron and Hur did for Moses during the Israelites' battle against the Amalekites. Aaron and Hur stood with Moses on the top of a hill, as they observed the battle. Moses had agreed to hold the staff of God in his hand for the duration of the battle (Exodus 17:9). The staff was a symbol of strength and guidance. The battle was noticeably affected by Moses' position or posture with this staff.

"So it came about when Moses held his hand up,
that Israel prevailed, and when he let his hand down,
Amalek prevailed.
Exodus 17:11

Aaron and Hur made the association of victory and defeat as it related to Moses' posture with the staff. They decided to do something: *"Do not withhold good from those to whom it is due, when it is in your power to do it"* (Proverbs 3:27).

"But Moses' hands were heavy. Then they took a stone and
put it under him, and he sat on it; and Aaron and Hur
supported his hands, one on one side and one on the other.
Thus his hands were ***steady*** *until the sun set.*
Exodus 17:12

Steady is the English translation for *emuwnah* which means "firmness, steadfastness; faithfulness, trust, honesty. It is derived from the word: *aman,* from which we get our word: *amen.* Aaron and Hur came along side of Moses to assist him in maintaining his posture as he held up the authority of God. Consider the effect of their help:

"So Joshua overwhelmed Amalek and his people
with the edge of the sword."
Exodus 17:13

Why should we use the Spoken Blessing?

Even if our hands are empty, our hearts are not.

Life Application:

Our fellow believers, even spiritual leaders, need physical and spiritual strength. Life is hard and the going gets tough. We can offer each other support. Many times needs are obvious. Someone's countenance, or posture and the words they speak serve as a clear signal for us to do something! Even if our hands are empty, our hearts are not. We have the River of Life flowing through and overflowing from us for the benefit of others. That life-giving Word can be spoken to refresh weary bones and uplift sagging spirits.

Why should we use the Spoken Blessing? It can change the results of a battle, even, the atmosphere and strength of a city:

"By the blessing of the upright a city is exalted,
but by the mouth of the wicked it is torn down."
Proverbs 11:11

Spoken Blessings can change someone's future:

Several years ago, I spoke to a women's group. I addressed the issue of using nicknames for our children and how detrimental some could be. At the close of my presentation, a mother of twin girls confided that one of her two-year-olds was very clumsy, and, in fact, she had been calling her that: "Clumsy." She was moved to repentance and change. No longer would this little girl grow up under such a burden, but would be strengthened and encouraged by her mother's blessings. I rejoiced for the lives that were changed.

Do not think lightly of the power of your words. Recall the truth revealed in Proverbs 18:21:

> *"Death and life are in the power of the tongue,*
> *and those who love it will eat its fruit."*

That two-year-old daughter would no longer have destructive words spoken against her. Robert S. McGee explained in *Father Hunger:* "No other human bond is as strong as the one between parent and child." As parents, we must not underestimate the power of our affection, attention and our words. Mr. McGee identified that "a major element of their (father and mother) parental duties was to pass along God's love to their growing children." "Of all the influences we will ever encounter—environment, personality, role models, peers, or whatever—nothing usually affects us as strongly as our parents. People can be brought up in harsh environments, experience severe poverty, run around with peers who drink or do drugs, yet overcome all these obstacles and go on to achieve great things. In almost every such case, these people attribute their success to parents who truly cared."

Over the years, I have sat in various waiting rooms and thumbed through magazines. Different stories have caught my attention. One such story tore at my heart. An adult male earnestly tried to reach his dying father's bedside. But he was minutes too late. He collapsed beside his father's lifeless body, weeping, uncontrollably. Minutes later, he looked into his father's face and begged: "Please, Daddy, just tell me that you love me . . . just tell me that you're proud of me. I love you, Daddy. Please, just say something." *Father Hunger* highlighted: "In the hearts of many men and women is a hollow place. We long for the blessing that only a father can give. Great numbers of adults continually struggle through life with unresolved emotional problems that can be traced back to the lack of a father's love. The emotional emptiness produced by father hunger can be destructive, powerful and long lasting. We all thrive on the love-signals we receive from our parents."

Even if you see your children acting in a clumsy, forgetful, or careless way, time and time again, don't start calling them names; don't begin projecting a negative expectation about their abilities. Exchange your frustration for a focus on what God wants them to become: graceful (or full of His grace), exercising a good memory, attentive and alert to the consequences of their actions. The Scriptures are full of examples of God's restoration for our lives:

Restoration honors God.

The Spirit of the Lord GOD is upon me,
because the LORD has anointed me
to bring good news to the afflicted;
He has sent me to bind up the brokenhearted,
to proclaim liberty to captives,
and freedom to prisoners;

to proclaim the favorable year of the LORD,
and the day of vengeance of our God;
to comfort all who mourn,
to grant those who mourn in Zion,
giving them a garland instead of ashes,
the oil of gladness instead of mourning,
the mantle of praise instead of a spirit of fainting.
So they will be called oaks of righteousness,
the planting of the LORD,
that He may be glorified."
Isaiah 61:1–3

Restoration honors God. When His people are blessed, others notice, just as Potiphar took note of God's blessing Joseph. God's people bless Him, also. Our son, whom I described in the Preface, was headed down a rocky road. Through the use of the Spoken Blessing, our attention was redirected to what God wanted to accomplish in his life. One of Peyton's lifetime goals is to serve as a medical missionary. On two different occasions during Peyton's teenage years, guest speakers at our church prophesied over him: "World-changer." At the writing of this book, Peyton is working towards becoming a Physician's Assistant. He has credited God with ENABLING him to comprehend and apply what he studies to the clinical work he encounters and to the numerous exams that he takes. Peyton has recognized the power and value of God's faithfully working within his life. God has coupled Peyton's compassionate heart with this vocation. A love for science has been exponentially multiplied and used. Peyton is right on track with his destiny . . . all to the glory of God.

Why should we use the Spoken Blessing?

It is a spiritual posture of confidence in God.

It is an expression of our faith. It is a spiritual posture of confidence in God.

Jesus taught His disciples about the expression of one's faith, the continual results that faith should produce and the importance of forgiveness.

"And on the next day, when they had departed from Bethany,
He became hungry.
And seeing at a distance a fig tree in leaf, He went to see if
perhaps He would find anything on it;
and when He came to it, He found nothing but leaves,
for it was not the season for figs.
And He answered and said to it,
'May no one ever eat fruit from you again!'
And His disciples were listening."
"And as they were passing by in the morning, they saw
the fig tree withered from the roots up.
And being reminded, Peter said to Him,
'Rabbi, behold, the fig tree which You cursed
has withered.'
And Jesus answered saying to them,
'Have faith in God. Truly I say to you,
whoever says to this mountain,
"Be taken up and cast into the sea,"
and does not doubt in his heart, but believes
that what he says is going to happen,

it shall be granted him.
Therefore I say to you, all things for which you pray
and ask, believe that you have received them,
and they shall be granted you.
And whenever you stand praying, forgive,
if you have anything against anyone;
so that your Father also who is in heaven
may forgive you your transgressions.'"
Mark 11:12–14, 20–25

Jesus had a need: He was hungry. Every day you will encounter people with needs: they are hungry for the Lord's presence in their lives. The leaves on this fig tree indicated that it was alive: the leaf is a symbol of life amidst prosperity or adversity. Many, many Christians, or "church-goers" are alive, but don't bear fruit for the benefit of others. They may attend church because it is the socially-acceptable thing to do or to have their personal needs met, but rarely do they assist or serve others. Their hearts are not seeking a submitted, intimate relationship with the Lord. Their focus is on themselves and not Him. 'Woe' to those who call themselves "Christians," but do not bear fruit for the Kingdom.

'Wow' to those who place their total trust and confidence in the Lord!:

"Blessed is the man who trusts in the LORD
And whose trust is the LORD.
For he will be like a tree planted by the water,
that extends its roots by a stream
and will not fear when the heat comes;
but its leaves will be green,
and it will not be anxious in a year of drought
nor cease to yield fruit."
Jeremiah 17:7–8

We are to yield fruit regardless of the external conditions. Why are we able to do that? How is it that heat and drought would not cause our fruit to cease?

. . . because their waters came from out of the sanctuary.

"And on the banks of the river on both its sides,
there shall grow all kinds of trees for food;
their leaf shall not fade nor shall their fruit fail
[to meet the demand].
Each tree shall bring forth new fruit every month,
[these supernatural qualities being]
because their waters came from out of the sanctuary.
And their fruit shall be for food and their leaves for healing."
Ezekiel 47:12 AMP

Why are we able to continually bear fruit? Our water, our sustenance comes from the sanctuary, the holy place. Who is our holy place?

"Now on the final and most important day of the Feast,
Jesus stood, and He cried in a loud voice,
If any man is thirsty, let him come to Me and drink!
He who believes in Me [who cleaves to
and trusts in and relies on Me]
as the Scripture has said,
From his innermost being shall flow[continuously] springs
and rivers of living water."
John 7:37, 38 AMP

We are the temple of the living God (II Corinthians 6:16). The life of Jesus, His Spirit, flows through us and continually produces fruit for the feeding and restoration of the people. In II Timothy 4:2, this analogy is continued:

"preach the word; be ready in season and out of season; reprove, rebuke, exhort, with great patience and instruction."

We are to proclaim Christ's victory to fallen spirits which is the act of Christ; acting in the likeness of Christ. There is an urgency in the phrase: "be ready." We are to never "go on leave." We are to continually bear fruit for the nurturing and renewal of others. As we serve others, we serve the Lord Jesus. Jesus was hungry and looking for fruit. Will He find fruit on our fig tree?

In Chapter 4, we discussed the importance of forgiveness. Jesus clearly addressed this need. As we forgive, we will be forgiven. Forgiveness feels so good. My heart always feels much cleaner, purer, when I have forgiven someone, or have asked for forgiveness. The enemy cannot bring words of condemnation against me. Doubt, fear and unbelief have no place within me. My spiritual posture is strong in the Lord. I can speak to those mountains and they will move. I can minister to others with authority, sharing God's glory, encouraging their intimate fellowship with the Lord as I speak blessings over them.

My spiritual posture is strong in the Lord.

By faith, you and I have the ability to call into being that which does not exist within a person's life:

"For this reason it is by faith, that it might be in accordance with grace, in order that the promise may be certain to all the descendants, not only to those who are of the Law, but also to those who are of the faith of Abraham,

141

who is the father of us all,
(as it is written, 'A FATHER OF MANY NATIONS
HAVE I MADE YOU')
in the sight of Him whom he believed, even God,
who gives life to the dead and calls into being that
which does not exist.
In hope against hope he believed,
in order that he might become, a father of many nations,
according to that which had been spoken,
'SO SHALL YOUR DESCENDANTS BE.'"
Romans 4:16–18

To believe is to become.

Another Old Testament figure exercised his faith and confidence in God. He trusted God's Almighty power to give life to the dead, calling into being that which did not exist.

"The hand of the LORD was upon me, and He brought
me out by the Spirit of the LORD and set me down in
the middle of the valley; and it was full of bones.
And He caused me to pass among them round about,
and behold, there were very many on the surface
of the valley; and lo, they were very dry.
And He said to me, 'Son of man, can these bones live?'
And I answered, 'O Lord GOD, Thou knowest.'
Again He said to me, 'Prophesy over these bones, and
say to them, "O dry bones, hear the word of the LORD."
Thus says the Lord GOD to these bones, "Behold, I will
cause breath to enter you that you may come to life.
And I will put sinews on you, make flesh grow back
on you, cover you with skin, and put breath in you
that you may come alive; and you will know that
I am the LORD.'"
So I prophesied as I was commanded; and as I prophesied,

there was a noise, and behold, a rattling; and the bones came
together, bone to its bone.
And I looked, and behold, sinews were on them, and flesh
grew, and skin covered them; but there was no breath
in them. Then He said to me, 'Prophesy to the breath,
prophesy, son of man, and say to the breath,
"Thus says the Lord GOD, 'Come from
the four winds, O breath,
and breathe on these slain, that they come to life.'"'
So I prophesied as He commanded me, and the breath
came into them, and they came to life, and stood
on their feet, an exceedingly great army."
Ezekiel 37:1–10

When you entwine your obedience and faith with the power of God's Holy Spirit, AN EXCEEDINGLY GREAT ARMY WILL ARISE TO THEIR FEET.

We encounter people whose hope has dried up, whose dreams are withered, whose zest for life is all but gone. They truly need resurrection power working in their lives.

Jesus is the Resurrection—

And Who is Jesus? The Word of God.

"In the beginning was the Word, and the Word was with God,
and the Word was God."
"And the Word became flesh, and dwelt among us,
and we beheld His glory, glory as of the only begotten
from the Father, full of grace and truth."
John 1:1,14

Ezekiel had to speak the Word of the Lord.

Ezekiel beheld the glory of the living God as he watched

those bones flying across the sky, being assembled into human structures. He beheld the glory of creation as God formed sinew, flesh and skin to cover those dry bones. This obedient prophet witnessed the resurrection power as the breath of life entered those bodies, causing color to flow, strength to surge and keen alertness to quicken them. What an awesome reward for faith, **spoken faith**, and obedience. Ezekiel had to speak the Word of the Lord.

When God hears you speaking His Word over someone, He honors His Word and the faith you are exercising.

"Then the LORD said to me, 'You have seen well, for I am watching over My word to perform it.'"
Jeremiah 1:12

God released a similar message through the prophet Isaiah:

"So shall My word be which goes forth from My mouth;
It shall not return to Me empty,
Without accomplishing what I desire,
And without succeeding in the matter for which I sent it."
Isaiah 55:11

From the beginning, the power of God's spoken word has been recognizable:

"Then God said, 'Let there be light;' and there was light."
Genesis 1:3

The spoken word has power to create life and light within a person, a city, a nation. God has given us the freedom to choose what we will speak and confess over ourselves, over others and over our surroundings. In Joshua 24:15, Joshua emphatically announced:

" . . . choose for yourselves today whom you will serve:
. . . but as for me and my house, we will serve the LORD."

Why should we use the Spoken Blessing?

1. **We are commanded to bless others.**

   "But I say to you who hear, love your enemies, do good to those who hate you, bless those who curse you, pray for those who mistreat you." Luke 6:27–28

2. **We are to serve the Lord all of our days.**

   " . . . Truly I say to you, to the extent that you did it to one of these brothers of Mine, even the least of them, you did it to Me." Matthew 25:40

3. **We have been given the ministry of reconciliation.**

   "For we are fellow workmen [joint promoters, laborers together] with and *for God;* you *are God's garden* and *vineyard* and *field under cultivation, [you are], God's building."* I Corinthians 3:9 AMP

4. **We can affect many lives for the Kingdom of God.**

   Jesus said to His disciples: *" . . . but you shall receive power when the Holy Spirit has come upon you; and you shall be My witnesses both in Jerusalem, and in all Judea and Samaria, and even to the remotest part of the earth."* Acts 1:8

My Blessing for You

*May the Lord's Holy Spirit flow through you, filling
every nook and cranny, meeting every need in your
life. May you know the height, breadth, width and
depth of His love for you. May you experience
His tender mercies which are new every morning.
May His joy fill you and overflow through you
onto others. May others look at you and see His
presence and glory. May others hear the words of
Christ as you speak blessings of encouragement
and truth; words which are seasoned with grace.
May you look upon the hills of your city
and notice that they are white and ripe for
harvest. May you not be ashamed of the gospel
of Jesus Christ; ready, in season and out,
to share the love of Christ with others.
In Jesus' Name, Amen.*

Journal of My Journey with the Spoken Blessing

What will you do this week to serve as God's minister of reconciliation?

_____

_____

_____

_____

_____ .

Write a blessing that addresses a specific need in someone's life. Speak it.

_____

_____

_____

_____

_____

_____

_____

_____ .

Identify needs within your church or body of believers of which you are a member. Write a blessing, then speak it over your fellow believers.

_____

_____

_____
_____
_____
_____
_____
_____
_____ .

Consider the city in which you live. Write, then speak that blessing over your city. Proclaim that blessing for 40 days.

_____
_____
_____
_____
_____
_____
_____
_____
_____
_____
_____ .

"The mouth of the righteous is a fountain of life. . . ."
Proverbs 10:11

Chapter 6

How Do I Assume the Spiritual Posture to Bless?

We assume our spiritual posture as we kneel at the feet of Jesus.

> *"Come, let us worship and bow down;*
> *Let us kneel before the LORD our Maker.*
> *For He is our God,*
> *And we are the people of His pasture, and the sheep*
> *of His hand.*
> *Today, if you would hear His voice,*
> *Do not harden your hearts . . ."*
> **Psalm 95:6–7**

In this passage, the Hebrew word used for *worship* is *shachah* which was not used in the general sense of worship, but specifically to bow down, to prostrate oneself as an act of respect before a superior being. This honor was not only to superiors, but also to equals, but especially in worshipping a deity. It meant to honor God with prayers. It was a way of showing submission.

Kara is the Hebrew word for *bow down*. It is defined: to bend (the knees), to kneel down, to sink down, to afflict, to grieve, to writhe in pain, to cower.

With an attitude of submission and honor and in a posture of humility, the worshipper would, also, *barak*—kneel down, bless, praise, be blessed, pray to, invoke, ask a blessing. Yes, when we are worshipping in the Lord's presence, we do praise and bless Him.

"I will extol Thee, my God, O King;
and I will bless [barak]
Thy name forever and ever.
Every day will I bless Thee,
And I will praise Thy name
forever and ever."
Psalm 145:1–2

When we are in His presence, we are blessed.

"The LORD is good to all:
And His mercies are over all His works."
"Thou dost open Thy hand,
And dost satisfy the desire of every living thing."
Psalm 145:9, 16

Speaking blessings over others can occur as a result of worshipping our Lord and King.

When we remain in His presence, we can invoke or put His name upon a situation or person, asking for and releasing a blessing. We bless others, in His Name. As we bless others, we celebrate and give glory to our God. Speaking blessings over others can occur as a result of worshipping our Lord and King.

"The LORD is near to all who call upon Him,
To all who call upon Him in truth.
He will fulfill the desire of those who fear Him;
He will also hear their cry, and will save them."

*"My mouth will speak the **praise** of the LORD;*
And all flesh will bless His holy name forever and ever."
Psalm 145:18, 19, 21

T hiliah is the Hebrew word used in verse 21 which is translated as *praise*. The meaning of *T hiliah* is laudation, a song of praise, glory, praiseworthiness, deeds which are worthy of praise.

T hiliah is traceable to *halal* which means to boast, to celebrate, to cause to shine. The phrase *hallelujah* calls for giving the glory to God. As we bless others, we bring to light the faithfulness of God. We celebrate His goodness and boast in who He is. Our blessings affirm God's deeds which are worthy to be praised.

When our triune being: body, soul and spirit, worships the Lord 'in spirit and truth,' the fullness of His love and mercy fills us to overflowing. It is from this overflow that our hearts are stirred with compassion to encourage, support and bless others—as Jesus blesses us. When blessing others 'for His sake' or 'in His Name,' we identify and help them identify that He is the only one worthy to be entrusted with our lives and our future.

"Do not trust in princes,
In mortal man, in whom there is no salvation."
"How blessed is he whose help is the God of Jacob,
Whose hope is in the LORD his God;"
Psalm 146:3, 5

"Let them praise the name of the LORD,
For His name alone is exalted;
His glory is above earth and heaven."
Psalm 148:13

Our lives must keep a posture of humility and an attitude of submission and honor before the One who blesses.

We must establish a deep-seated trust in Him.

In Psalm 91, there is a beautiful relationship expressed between the worshipper and his Lord:

"He who dwells in the shelter (secret place) of the Most High
Will abide in the shadow of the Almighty.
I will say to the LORD, 'My refuge and my fortress,
My God, in whom I trust!'"

God responds to the worshipper:

*"Because he has **loved** Me, therefore I will deliver him;*
I will set him securely on high, because he has known My name.
He will call upon Me, and I will answer him;
I will be with him in trouble;
I will rescue him, and honor him.
With a long life I will satisfy him,
And let him behold My salvation.'"
Psalm 91:1–2, 14–16

In God's response, He reveals several 'cause and effect' relationships:

Cause	Effect
1. person *loves* God	1. God delivers him
2. person knows God's names (has personal experience with and knowledge of God)	2. God establishes him with authority
3. person calls upon God	3. God hears his plea and answers him
4. person is in trouble	4. God is with him, not leaving him
5. person needs help	5. God rescues him
6. person needs edifying	6. God honors him
7. person wants to live for God and wants His sovereignty in his life	7. God fulfills his desires
8. person wants to see His salvation	8. God shows him His help, deliverance, salvation, victory, welfare, prosperity

When a person *loves (chashaq)* God, he is attached to Him, he takes pleasure and delight in Him, he is joined together with Him, cleaving and adhering to Him. It is a love that will not let go. Thus, if this person is so close to God, he can't help but be delivered, rescued and extricated from a 'hot spot.' Jesus escaped a crowd who wanted to kill Him, because His time to die had not yet come (John 8:59; 10:31, 39). I do not disregard the martyrs (past, present and future) who gave (and will give) their earthly lives to serve a heavenly king. As Stephen was being stoned, he looked upward into the presence of His Lord. His Lord extricated or drew him out of that situation. Stephen's earthly body died, but his spirit soared into heaven (Acts 7:54–60). Even when we give our earthly lives for a heavenly purpose, it is not an indication that the enemy has won or that God has forsaken us. Just the contrary . . . the enemy lost us at the precise moment when we gave our lives to Christ.

The giving of our lives occurs before the time of our physical death.

"Greater love has no one than this, that one *lay down his life for his friends.*" (John 15:13; I John 3:16).

The love we have for Jesus, causes us to adhere to Him and do what He did . . . sacrifice Himself. When believers reach this level of consecration and love, they will bless and curse not their neighbor . . . letting all blessings flow.

Join with me in a prayer of repentance for not loving Jesus to this degree:

Lord Jesus, please forgive me for not loving You in the depths of my being. Please forgive me for wanting all of Your goodness, mercy and grace without the total sacrifice of my life.
Forgive me for presuming upon Your grace.
Please forgive me for not adhering to and immersing myself in Your presence.
Forgive me for allowing other things to take precedence in my life.
Lord, I want to establish You as my life, my source, my sustenance, the One in Whom I trust for everything.
Jesus, I humble and submit myself, all of me, to You.
In Your Name, I pray. Amen.

Oh, Father, teach us now, I pray. Teach us the humility and submissiveness of Jesus. Forgive me, Father, of all haughtiness in my spirit. I crucify the attitude of pride. Oh, Lord, let us become the oil that flows out of our broken, alabaster box. The oil that costs us everything. . . . our entire life's earnings, everything we have built our lives upon. . . . we pour it at Your feet. Take it all, Lord, so we have nothing left of ourselves . . . so

You can fill us up with only You . . . Your nature and character. A broken and contrite heart, You will not despise.

Humility, submission and love for God provides knowledge of Him, experiencing the fullest dimensions of His name, His character.

Yada is to know . . . if we know the names of God, we have spent much time at His feet and in His presence. We have walked and talked with Him. We have watched His ways and observed His workings. We have experienced His different names and know that we can call upon those attributes when in need.

Sit at the feet of Jesus in quiet *repose,* carefully weighing and considering His Word. *Repose* refers to resting from work, travel, exercise, etc. It means that you are depending upon or relying on someone or something beyond yourself. Your mind is at peace and free from the worries of the world.

As you discipline your mind to overcome the worries of the world, may Jesus reward you by sharing His intimacies with you (Proverbs 3:32). Allow His truth, His Word, to become the authority over your life; the rule of your conduct. Join the ranks of those biblical giants who have assumed a similar posture:

> *"Then David the king went in and sat before the LORD*
> *and said, 'Who am I, O LORD God,*
> *and what is my house that Thou*
> *hast brought me this far?'"*
> **I Chronicles 17:16**

Speaking of his heritage and thorough training, Paul declared:

> *"I am a Jew, born in Tarsus of Cilicia*
> *but reared in this city. At the feet of Gamaliel I was*
> *educated according to the strictest care in the Law*
> *of our fathers, being ardent [even a zealot] for God,*

as all of you are today."
Acts 22:3 AMP

Allow your heart to be stirred to embrace His joys, His sorrows, His goals, His Kingdom vision.

Seek the broader dimensions of the teachings and parables of Jesus. Read between the lines. Dig deeper for the treasures hidden beneath the surface. Ask Jesus to explain His teachings to you (Mark 4:33–34). Value His gemstones of truth, examining their multi-faceted surfaces. Look into the light of His glory as did the Emmaus Road disciples. As they intently listened to their dinner guest explain the Scriptures, their demeanor changed and their perspective of Jesus turned 180°. Allow your heart to be stirred to embrace His joys, His sorrows, His goals, His Kingdom vision. Faith in Jesus' eternal purpose was birthed within their hearts that night. After listening and learning from Jesus, these disciples' vision changed from being 'near-sighted' to 'far-sighted;' for they could see far into the future of God's Kingdom. They were comforted and encouraged by this new perspective; not allowing the present circumstances to discourage or hinder them.

Upon listening to Jesus, the Emmaus Road disciples openly expressed their faith in Him. Such faith pleases God. Two other disciples had spent time at the feet of Jesus: Mary and Martha. Mary and Martha expressed faith and expectation in Jesus as they called for His help when their beloved brother, Lazarus, was seriously ill. After the death of her brother, Martha heard of Jesus' arrival at Bethany. Martha arose from her weeping to greet her Lord and to openly confess who He was for her and for the world.

" . . . I have believed [I do believe] that You are the Christ
[the Messiah, the Anointed One], the Son of God,
[even He] Who was to come into the world.
[It is for Your coming that the world has waited.] "
John 11:27 AMP

We must remain humble and submissive to Him, honoring His omniscience.

Martha may not have understood Jesus' delay in coming to their aid, but she was not deterred from greeting Him with warm hospitality and affirmation of her faith in Him. Martha teaches us something very important here: when we call upon the name of Jesus, expecting Him to respond in a certain way, and He doesn't, we should not assume that we are being denied an answer or that He isn't interested in our concern. Our faith in Him should not suffer, nor be shaken. We should continue to openly confess, as Martha did, who Jesus is for us and to the world. Our prayers and our blessings should remain focused on Him, His nature and His purpose. As in the death of Lazarus and in the delay of Jesus' arrival, we must remember that God's ways are higher than ours; His understanding more complete, His timing more perfect. We must remain humble and submissive to Him, honoring His omniscience.

While in our finite minds and limited understanding of His ways, we may not grasp the totality of the *task at hand,* we can be confident that eternal destinies are being developed and the Lord's salvation is being accomplished. Our belief in Him and outward confession of our faith will open 'doors of opportunity' for us to witness the glory of God and for others to enter into salvation.

. . . if you believe, you will see the glory of God . . .

"Jesus said to her {Martha}, 'Did I not say to you,
if you believe, you will see the glory of God?'
And so they removed the stone. And Jesus raised His eyes,
and said, 'Father, I thank Thee that Thou heardest Me.
And I knew that Thou hearest Me always;
but because of the people standing around I said it,
that they may believe that Thou didst send Me.'
And when He had said these things, He
cried out with a loud voice,
'Lazarus, come forth.'
He who had died came forth, bound
hand and foot with wrappings,
and his face was wrapped around with a cloth.
Jesus said to them, 'Unbind him, and let him go.'
Many therefore of the Jews, who had come to Mary
and beheld what He had done, believed in Him."
John 11:40–45

Trust God to operate within the fullest dimension of eternity.

To reveal the glory of God and for the work of salvation, Jesus delayed His response to the call for help. Delay does not equate to denial. Take note that many Jews had come to comfort and mourn with Mary and Martha. These friends would have had no reason to be with Lazarus' sisters if Jesus had healed and rescued Lazarus from death. By delaying His arrival, Jesus performed a resurrection miracle before the eyes and hearts of these Jewish friends which led to their belief in Him. Trust God to operate within the fullest dimension of eternity. Our faith must not be shaken, but confident in God's perfect plan of action within our world. Faith exercised and expressed can result in the resurrection of 'dead' areas within lives as we release blessings of truth and life over people. We can "unbind" them and free them from the grave cloths of defeat and discouragement. New life, new hope, new optimism will replace death and decay. Their attitudes and outlook will no longer "stink," but will emit the sweet fragrance of the presence of the Lord ruling and reigning in their lives.

Recall with me the story in Mark 11 that describes Jesus cursing the fig tree and His disciples marveling that His words carried such power. He began a valuable lesson which can assist us in assuming the spiritual posture for speaking blessings.

"And Jesus answered saying to them, 'Have faith in God.'"
Mark 11:22

Faith is the English translation of the Greek word, *pistis,* which means being persuaded; faith; believe. In general, it implies such a knowledge of, assent to, and confidence in certain divine truths, especially those of the Gospel, as produces good works.

That definition tells me that our faith in God should result in doing good. The Word reminds us of the importance of our lively, active faith in Christ:

"Do not withhold good from those to whom it is due, when it is in your power to do it."
Proverbs 3:27

" . . . I will show you my faith by my works."
James 2:18

Pistis relates to miraculous faith or that faith in Christ to which, when the Gospel was first spread, the gift of miracles was added. The working of miracles became an additional consequence of an active, power-filled faith.

Paul prayed that such a faith would be *developed* within the Colossian believers:

> *" . . . we have not ceased to pray for you and to ask*
> *that you may be filled with the knowledge of His*
> *will in all spiritual wisdom and understanding,*
> *so that you may walk in a manner worthy of the Lord,*
> *to please Him in all respects, bearing fruit in every*
> *good work and increasing in the knowledge of God;*
> *strengthened with all power, according to His glorious might,*
> *for the attaining of all steadfastness and patience;*
> *joyously giving thanks to the Father, who has qualified us*
> *to share in the inheritance of the saints in light."*
> **Colossians 1:9–12**

To assume the posture to use the Spoken Blessing effectively, we need to:

1. **"be filled with the knowledge of His will in all spiritual wisdom and understanding"** . . . Just as Jacob spoke appropriate blessings over his sons, we are to seek and listen for wisdom from God's Spirit as we bless others.

2. **"walk in a manner worthy of the Lord".** . . . .Bring God honor by redirecting someone's focus and attention back to Him.

3. **"please Him in all respects"** . . . Be obedient to His Word as He instructs us to bless and not curse people. Share the cup of forgiveness. And do not neglect doing good and sharing, for with such sacrifices God is pleased (Hebrews 13:16).

4. **"bear fruit in every good work"** . . . The fruit of the

righteous is a tree of life, and he who is wise wins souls (Proverbs 11:30).

5. **"increase in the knowledge of God"** . . . As we study and seek to understand the nature of God, we will know how He desires to bless others. Study Jesus. Carefully examine His interactions with people and consider the outcome. Ask Him to relate each situation to your life.

6. **"be strengthened with all power, according to His glorious might"** . . . As God did special miracles through the hands of Paul (Acts 19:11), He will enable us to release and build up greater measures of faith and works within others.

7. **"attain all steadfastness and patience"** . . . We must press on toward the goal for the prize of the upward call of God in Christ Jesus (Philippians 3:14). Our blessings should encourage others to do the same. We are to become secure and established in our faith; patient in our daily walk.

8. **"joyously give thanks to the Father"** . . . Our blessings should remind fellow believers to bless, praise and thank our heavenly Father (Psalm 145).

Take note of the last phrase of Colossians 1:12: *"who has qualified us to share in the inheritance of the saints in light."* The act of confessing with our mouths that Jesus is our Lord allows us to step into an eternal inheritance. We must express our faith in Him.

"that if you confess with your mouth Jesus as Lord, and believe in your heart that God raised Him from the dead, you shall be saved; for with the heart man believes, resulting in righteousness, and with the mouth he confesses, resulting in salvation."
Romans 10:9–10

I am continually reminded of how our choice to believe in Christ and our willingness to confess that faith affects, not only ourselves, but others. On many occasions, I have felt prompted by God's Spirit to speak a blessing over a customer in our store. Most often, I witness a visible change in their countenance. Many times, they will say: "Thank you, I needed that." Their thanks is not casual or superficial, but one of deep gratitude. I can see it in their eyes as they look at me with a different intensity. By God's Spirit, I minister to their spirit. Our spirits are eternal: they existed before we were given an earthly body and will exist after this earthly body dies. This underscores the importance of calling 'deep unto deep,' spirit summoning spirit . . . . our eternity, their eternity lies ahead.

Recall the consequence of blessing others as identified in I Peter 3:9—*"for you were called for the very purpose that you might inherit a blessing."* Over and over and over again, God's Word reiterates the correlation between our actions and our eventual inheritance.

"Whatever you do, do your work heartily,
as for the Lord rather than for men;
knowing that from the Lord you will receive the reward
of the inheritance. It is the Lord Christ whom you serve."
Colossians 3:23–24

As we grow in our understanding of God's message about the Spoken Blessing, we must translate it into faith-filled action. Such action is identified in Mark 11:23:

"Truly I say to you, whoever says to this mountain,
'Be taken up and cast into the sea . . .'"

A person must speak blessings with authority. We must be confident in God's power Who works within us, namely, His Holy Spirit. We must recognize the significance and importance of our work here on earth, in this life time, as it relates to the future: individually and corporately. **We must embrace a larger picture that incorporates eternity.** {Please read Dr. Bruce Wilkinson's *A Life God Rewards—Why Everything You Do Today Matters Forever.* Gain a new perspective on eternity.}

We can not be spineless men and women of the faith. In fact, those are opposing ideas. If we are committed believers and confess faith in the Lord, we will walk uprightly, holding our heads up high, shoulders firmly set, backbones straight and strong. As we gain the revelation of the kingdom of God Who lives within us and the kingdom in which we live, we will rule and reign with Jesus; confident and assertive.

Each of us needs the other in our service to the Lord.

Why is grabbing hold of this 'larger picture' so vital to our "pressing on toward the goal for the prize?" Life has its "pressing" moments or seasons. Olives produce oil and grapes produce juice when they are pressed and crushed. "Crushing circumstances" are not comfortable. But, as we are "pressed," we must "press" on towards a deeper, more intimate relationship with our Lord. As God gives us an understanding of what is happening and why, we must respond with submission and repentance. In honor and reverence to Jesus, we can take our "pressed oil" or "extracted juice" and pour it on His feet. There are Christians who become angry at God for different reasons. Generally speaking, these people refuse to be "crushed" for the sake of spiritual growth and a deeper walk. Their hearts are hardened to His Spirit and their necks are stiffened to His correction. They become 'bitter' instead of 'better.' They choose to focus on their present, instead of their future. Cal and I have walked through "crushing" times. On our knees and before the

Lord, we have 'panned' for the golden nuggets of truth, allowing the water of His Word to wash away the dirt and debris of disappointments. Our faith in God's BIGGER picture was at the forefront of our minds and hearts. Yes, we had to clean up our hearts through repentance and renew our spirits by His Word. We had friends who prayed for us, blessed and exhorted us in our faith. No man is an island. When asked for instruction in prayer, Jesus stressed to His disciples the idea of the community of believers: *"**Our** Father who art in heaven . . . give **us** this day . . . forgive **us** . . . as **we** also have . . . do not lead **us** . . . deliver **us**. . . ."* (Matthew 6:9–13). Each of us needs the other in our service to the Lord.

We are the Body of Christ. Our physical bodies must remain aligned to function properly. Many health problems develop when we get out of alignment. There are highly-trained, medical professionals who help us realign our skeletal structures for optimal health. We can assist one another, within the Body of Christ, to become spiritually realigned and to maintain this proper posture.

We need this spiritual posture to enable us to rule and reign with Jesus.

Jesus equipped His disciples for His kingdom work:

"And He called the twelve together, and gave them power and authority over all the demons and to heal diseases.
And He sent them out to proclaim the kingdom of God,
and to perform healing."
Luke 9:1–2

There was an impartation of power and authority from

Jesus to His disciples. Jesus challenged them to think and see beyond what they had witnessed while serving Him:

> *"Truly, truly I say to you, he who believes in Me,*
> *the works that I do shall he do also;*
> *and greater works than these shall he do;*
> *because I go to the Father.*
> *And whatever you ask in My name, that will I do,*
> *that the Father may be glorified in the Son.*
> *If you ask Me anything in My name, I will do it."*
> ***John 14:12–14***

We are to "have faith" in the M A G N I T U D E of God and the V A S T N E S S of His kingdom work. Jesus' disciples had witnessed healing, deliverance, resurrection, blessing, re-creation, compassion, mercy, forgiveness, etc. Jesus expected and called His disciples to exponentially multiply His work. We are called to do no less.

A side note of interest: Jesus explained to His disciples: *"Whatsoever you ask in my name that will I do,"* (John 14:13). He expressed the importance of their prayers being conformable to His nature and character; to the actions His disciples observed Him doing while on earth. Our blessings should follow suite. As we speak blessings based upon the Word, who is Jesus, He will respond to those blessings. He desires to execute His Word within the lives of people.

Let's continue with our original passage found in Mark 11:22–23:

> *"Have faith in God.*
> *Truly I say to you, whoever says to this mountain,*
> *'Be taken up and cast into the sea,'*
> ***and does not doubt in his heart,"***

Doubt means: to be distinguished or divided in one's mind.

Doubting or not doubting is related to our confidence in God and in His ultimate will for our lives and those of others. *"Therefore, do not throw away your confidence, which has a great reward"* (Hebrews 10:35). Jesus addressed the doubt and faithlessness in His disciple, Thomas, who would not believe in His resurrection until he could see and touch Jesus, in person. *"Because you have seen Me, have you believed? Blessed are they who did not see, and yet believed"* (John 20:29). God truly desires and is eager to encourage His divine nature and image to be multiplied across the world. Doubt can have no place in us. It cannot hold any power over our faith.

Continuing with Mark 11:23:

"and does not doubt in his heart,
but believes that what he says is going to happen,"

Pisteuo is the Greek word which is translated as *believes*. *Pisteuo* is derived from *pistis* which refers to *faith* or *belief*. Once again, *faith* is the focal point. Being confident in what we believe is essential. Confidence has its reward. Jesus questioned His disciples about the basis of their faith in Him:

"He said to them, 'But who do you say that I am?'
And Simon Peter answered and said,
'Thou art the Christ, the Son of the living God.'
And Jesus answered and said to him,
*'**Blessed** are you, Simon Barjona, because flesh and blood*
did not reveal this to you, but My Father who is in heaven.
And I also say to you that you are Peter and upon this rock
I will build My church; and the gates of Hades
shall not overpower it.'"
Matthew 16:15–18

Simon Peter was *blessed, makarios,* filled up, fully satisfied by the presence of God through Christ Jesus. As Jesus recognized the spiritual state of Peter, He knew that there was no doubt or anxiety within Peter's heart or mind. Having God's rule in His life, Peter was able to state, with confidence, his belief that Jesus was The Anointed One and His Anointing. Upon this foundational belief, Jesus would build His church. Jesus knew He could accomplish His kingdom work within a life so totally convinced of this fact. With this confidence, we are to speak blessings, believing what we speak will happen. Every believer has an anointing given by the presence of the Spirit of Christ.

"But you have been anointed by
[you hold a sacred appointment from, you
have been given an unction from]
the Holy One, and you all know [the Truth]
or you know all things."
I John 2:20 AMP

My trusted 'Webster' explains the word **unction**: "a quality or manner of utterance, especially in dealing with religious themes, that is fervent and earnest, or meant to express or arouse deep spiritual feeling." As the Spirit of the Lord stirs within us, teaching, directing and moving us in His truth and compassion, we will not be able to keep our mouths from pronouncing His blessings upon people. As we are trained by His Spirit, fervent words of encouragement will be spoken with faith that it will happen. Our words of faith spoken over someone else will serve to encourage us.

"So faith comes from hearing, and hearing
from the Word of Christ."
Romans 10:17

Life Application:

There are times when a child is struggling with an issue and the parents feel his pain. When the parents speak blessings over the child, parents and child are strengthened because they are reminded of God's presence and interest. All are reassured that it is God's loving-kindness and faithfulness that will provide victory over the challenge.

"May you watch as God does exceeding abundantly beyond all
that you ask or think, according to the power
of His Spirit who works within you.
May God's favor surround you like a shield.
May the Lord be your Good Shepherd, caring and
providing for your every need.
May you call upon the name of Jesus when you need help.
In Jesus' Name, Amen.

If a spouse, friend or co-worker has been harassed by demeaning words spoken by others, it is vital to their victory for you to continually speak blessings of affirmation and encouragement. Old thoughts and perspectives must be washed away and new outlooks must be imparted. At times this can become a battle that must be fought. Unfortunately, some people, i.e.: members of our family, long-time friends and superiors continually berate our loved one. Such continual harsh judgments often create a defeated and inferior mentality within our spouse or friend. These condemning words must be confronted with God's truth. By the authority and command of Christ, we are to *love* others. On the home front, husbands are to *agapao* their wives. They are to love their wives, indicating a direction of the husband's will. Remember the words of Paul found in Ephesians 5:25–27:

*"Husbands, **love** your wives, just as*
Christ also loved the church
and gave Himself up for her; that He might sanctify her,
having cleansed her by the washing of water with the word,
that He might present to Himself the church in all her glory,
having no spot or wrinkle or any such thing;
but that she should be holy and blameless."

Husbands are to extend great compassion to their wives, discovering how to lovingly encourage them in all the seasons of life through which they walk. Husbands and wives must be careful not to destroy each other with name-calling and destructive words.

Wives, we must learn how to forgive the offenses that come from our husbands. Now, be honest. Offenses from our husbands are, often, some of the hardest ones to "get over." A key element to our emotional, physical, and spiritual health is directly connected to our forgiveness. Our forgiveness is directly related to our being able to bless and not curse our husbands. Our blessing them affects our inheritance in eternity.

Fellow wives and fellow mothers, we have a great responsibility to the building up of our homes:

"The wise woman builds her house,
But the foolish tears it down with her own hands."
Proverbs 14:1

The building up or the tearing down is in the power of our hands and our mouths. Our husbands need affirmation. They need our admiration according to Dr. Willard F. Harley, Jr., author of *His Needs, Her Needs*. Dr. Harley suggests that "when a woman tells a man she thinks he's wonderful, that inspires him to achieve more. He sees himself as capable of handling new responsibilities and perfecting skills far above those of his present level. That inspiration helps him prepare for the responsibilities of life. Admiration not only motivates, it also rewards the husband's existing achievements. For some men—those with fragile self-images—admiration also helps them believe in themselves. While criticism causes men to become defensive, admiration energizes and motivates them. A man expects—and needs—his wife to be his most enthusiastic fan. He draws confidence from her support and can usually achieve far more with her encouragement."

Wives, our husbands need our blessings, our faith-filled words of God's Truth spoken over, around, before and behind them. Even when we speak about them to others, our words must always honor and esteem them. Our husbands should be able to safely trust us with their honor and their every need as is described in Proverbs 31:11–12 AMP:

"The heart of her husband trusts in her confidently
and relies on and believes in her securely,
so that he has no lack of [honest] gain or need
of [dishonest] spoil. She comforts,
encourages, and does him only good as
long as there is life within her."

Wives, our words can affect who our husbands are and who they shall become. Let us carefully consider God's perspective concerning our husbands. Do not condone or agree with attitudes which condemn or demean "husbands" or "men." We must not remain silent when other females criticize the male gender. They are attacking the image of God.

We are to honor the image of Christ that dwells within our husbands and our children.

Speaking blessings over our husbands honors them as the co-laborers in Christ that they are. We are to honor the image of Christ that dwells within our husbands *and* our children. As wives and mothers, we are to *build up our homes*. Dr. Harley identified that low self-esteem has been one of the most common problems his clients have had to overcome. He explained that this low self-esteem begins very early, in the home during childhood. This fact underlines the necessity of our watching our words. . . . holding our tongues, even, biting them if necessary. Words can be so hurtful, but so comforting and motivating, when they are *seasoned with salt* (Colossians 4:6). Remember, salt is a *preservative*. We are to *preserve* our family's honor and image.

Likewise, we can (it is a choice we make) play an important part in the sanctification, the setting apart, of fellow believers for the work of God's kingdom. We can remind others of the authority that God has over their lives and over His world. We can challenge them to reach higher; to dig deeper, discovering the richer elements of life. We can extend compassion for their failures, while exhorting them to a purer walk of holiness. Cleansing one's mind and sanctifying one's thoughts can take time and require repetition. There is a joy and a reward for serving others.

Jesus said, *"For whoever gives you a cup of water to drink because of your name as followers of Christ, truly I say to you, he shall not lose his reward."*
Mark 9:41

The principle of the cleansing and restorative power of God's Word is evident and profound. People need to hear, over and over and over again, who they are in Christ. We have the ability and the anointing to build up and establish a firm foundation of faith, hope and love within others as we speak blessings over them.

God has placed a seed of greatness within every person. We can help it to grow and develop into a tree of righteousness that bears good fruit.

Jesus continued His explanation in Mark 11:23. . . . .

*"but believes that what he says is going to happen, **it shall be granted him.**"*

It is imperative that we trust God to act on our behalf and on the behalf of others. Trust God's Word when it declares:

"but just as it is written,
'things which eye has not seen and ear has not heard,
and which have not entered the heart of man,
all that God has prepared for those who love Him.'
For to us God revealed them through the Spirit;
for the Spirit searches all things, even the depths of God."
I Corinthians 2:9–10

Assuming the spiritual posture to bless others requires a humble and contrite heart, a life totally submitted to Jesus' Lordship, faith in Who He is, and confidence in the authority and power His has given you.

My Blessing for You

May you kneel at the feet of Jesus. May
you allow Him to take you by the hand,
His omnipotent hand, and set your feet on
the solid foundation of faith in Him.
As He causes your faith to flourish, may you

take steps to accomplish His mighty work for the furtherance of His Kingdom. May you walk with a heart of submission, operating with an understanding of your authority and command to bless. May you continually bless the God of your salvation, encouraging others to do the same. **In Jesus' Name, Amen.**

Journal of My Journey with the Spoken Blessing

What do you need to learn at the feet of Jesus?

_____

_____

_____

_____ .

What area(s) in your life has yet to be totally submitted to His authority?

_____

_____

_____

_____ .

Identify the level of trust in God that you desire to assume. What must you do to get there?

_____

_____

_____

_____ .

Describe the effect God has recently had on your life. Explain the situation and His response.

_____

_____
_____
_____
_____
_____.

Recount a situation in which God's response to you appeared to be delayed. When and how did He answer?

_____
_____
_____
_____
_____.

This week, how will you show others your faith by your works?

_____
_____
_____
_____.

"And my God shall supply all your needs
according to His riches in glory in Christ Jesus."
Philippians 4:19

Chapter 7

Interning with the Spoken Blessing

Are you ready to begin using the Spoken Blessing? Are you willing to put your approach to life to the test? Carefully consider the following story from Luke 7:

> *"And it came about soon afterwards, that*
> *He went to a city called Nain;*
> *and His disciples were going along with Him,*
> *accompanied by a large multitude.*
> *Now as He approached the gate of the city, behold, a dead man*
> *was being carried out, the only son of his*
> *mother, and she was a widow;*
> *and a sizeable crowd from the city was with her.*
> *And when the Lord saw her, He felt compassion for her,*
> *and said to her, 'Do not weep.'*
> *And He came up and touched the coffin;*
> *and the bearers came to a halt.*
> *And He said, 'Young man, I say to you, arise!'*
> *And the dead man sat up, and began to speak. And Jesus*
> *gave him back to his mother.*
> *And fear gripped them all, and they began glorifying God,*
> *saying, 'A great prophet has arisen among us!' and*
> *'God has visited His people!'"*
> ***Luke 7:11–16***

He did not want to fix a problem.

There were two crowds that day. The atmosphere around each was distinctively different. There was an air of excitement and anticipation surrounding Jesus and His disciples. A cloud of doom and gloom hovered over the mourners. If we had been there, of which crowd would we have been a part? Which outlook on life do we embrace? Are we an excited, expectant, faith-filled follower of the Lord? Or, are we forlorn, hopeless, and dejected? Are we in a 'survival mode?' Does our future *appear* as bleak as this widow's? This woman was not only a widow, but her last means of survival had just died. Her future did not appear promising. Imagine that the winds of despair were blinding her from seeing her future in a positive way. Her visual impairment was caused by a 'short-sighted' view of life. But then, God appeared on the scene. God in the flesh, our Lord Jesus, was moved with compassion. Jesus gave 'sight' to this 'blinded' widow-mother as He firmly instructed her to stop weeping, crying and carrying on. The word, compassion, indicates that the total person feels compassion. Jesus' entire nature responded to this widow. He did not want to fix a problem. He desired a change in this woman's approach to her circumstances; to her life. Jesus did not want her to continue in the 'woe is me' frame of mind. Restoration was needed. Jesus did more than restore life and provision in the natural sense. Awe and reverence for His Heavenly Father gripped this crowd, not just the widow. Their spiritual focus was changed. Their awareness of God's working among them was heightened. Hope was restored; hope was multiplied.

Will Jesus find it necessary to say to us:

"Stop your negative, faithless approach to life. Stop the doubt-filled and 'woe is me' confessions of your mouth. What's in your mouth comes from your heart."

His Word declares:

"Death and life are in the power of the tongue,
And those who love it will eat its fruit."
Proverbs 18:21

James 3:6 clearly identifies the power of the tongue:

"And the tongue is a fire, the very world
of iniquity; the tongue is set
among our members as that which defiles the entire body,
and sets on fire the course of our life, and is set on fire by hell."

Take note of—'sets on fire the course of our life.' Our tongue directs our focus and the path we follow in life. Whoa! That's why Jesus wanted the widow to change her woe-filled outlook. He knew He had a better future for her, if she would stop and change her direction; her mental and emotional attitudes.

"But no one can tame the tongue; it is a
restless evil and full of deadly poison.
With it we bless our Lord and Father; and with it we curse men,
who have been made in the likeness of God;
from the same mouth come both blessing and cursing.
My brethren, these things ought not to be this way.
Does a fountain send out from the same
opening both fresh and bitter water?"
James 3:8–11

"For with Thee is the fountain of life;
In Thy light we see light."
Psalm 36:9

When we look at life through the eyes of Jesus, we can see "light at the end of the tunnel." The hearts that have been darkened by doubt and despair must choose to allow His fountain of life to flood through them, washing away the death and decay of pessimism. As we speak blessings with great compassion, we can touch the dead areas within someone with the Word of Life. We can assist them in returning to their God-appointed vocation and destiny.

When we look at life through the eyes of Jesus . . .

Jesus said:

> " . . . I came that they may have and enjoy
> life, and have it in abundance
> [to the full, till it overflows]."
> **John 10:10 AMP**

Do you want this 'abundant life?' Follow the Lord as He declared:

> "For the Lord GOD helps Me,
> Therefore I am not disgraced;
> Therefore, I have **set** My face like flint,
> And I know that I shall not be **ashamed**."
> **Isaiah 50:7**

We walk in the direction of our focus.

To **set,** suwm, means to establish, to erect, to plant, to put, to appoint; to set aside for a special purpose. If our face is set, it is firmly focused–focused on our God in whom we trust. We walk in the direction of our focus. We will not be **ashamed,** buwsh, disappointed, deceived or confused. We will not suffer the shame of utter defeat. God is our very present help in times of trouble. The fiery trials of life must not distract us or force us into a lowly "survival mode" of thinking and speaking. We must not allow those trials to interfere with God's purpose for our lives and His plans for others. Psalm 23:1 declares that the LORD is our Shepherd, we shall not want. That important principle is the launching pad for our faith. He shall accomplish exceeding abundantly more than we could ever ask or think (Ephesians 3:20). That's the baseline of our lives. Our authority, dominion and power in His Name, supercedes the basics of life. We ARE over-comers by the Blood of the Lamb! Our life has a purpose and it's *not* just to survive.

Even when Job lost all of his sons and daughters, his servants, his livestock, even his health, he "did not sin with his lips" (Job 2:10). He did not blame God, instead, Job worshipped God and blessed His name (Job 1:20–22).

As we set our face, focused on the Lord, we direct our mouth to speak blessings, not curses. We will become like David who explained his inward resolve:

*"I have **purposed** that my **mouth** will not **transgress.** "*
Psalm 17:3d

David carefully considered and planned that the noticeable manifestation of his character and disposition would not violate God's law, nor go beyond it. When I say something that causes pain to others, I am indeed regretful. My remorse causes me to meditate on why I said what I did, trying to understand myself and my attitude, so I can make changes. I attempt to find the root of the problem. Remove the root, the bad fruit dries up. I have to be very honest with myself; emotionally separated and analytical. When I have offended someone, I apologize and ask for their forgiveness. I truly desire the song of David to be in my heart and on my lips:

"Let the words of my mouth and the meditation of my heart
Be acceptable in Thy sight, O LORD,
my rock and my Redeemer."
Psalm 19:14

How can we keep our way pure and acceptable in God's sight?

> " . . . *By keeping it according to Thy word.*
> *With all my heart I have sought Thee;*
> *Do not let me **wander** from Thy commandments.*
> *Thy word I have treasured in my heart,*
> *That I may not sin against Thee."*
> **Psalm 119:9–11**

Read the same passage in the *Amplified Bible:*

> " . . . *By taking heed and keeping watch [on himself] according*
> *to Your word [conforming his life to it].*
> *With my whole heart have I sought You,*
> *inquiring for and of You and yearning for You;*
> *O let me not **wander** or step aside*
> *[either in ignorance or willfully]*
> *from Your commandments.*
> *Your word have I laid up in my heart,*
> *that I might not sin against You."*

To **wander**, *shagah,* is to waiver, to go astray, to err, to transgress, to cause to wander, to sin through ignorance. One thing that causes us to stray away from God's commands is the inability to fend off evil talk.

To 'fend off' is to ward off, turn aside, or repel. Recall that evil talk is full of fear, doubt and unbelief.

This is an area of sin into which many people *wander.* We listen to and agree with many attitudes and words of people who spew out negative, woe-filled expectations. {Examples: "Well, if it's not one thing, it's another." This is often spoken after several 'bad' things have happened. "Everything happens to me in threes. I wonder what else is going to happen!" "I can't seem to do anything right." "He's never there when you need him."

"Yeah, I always come up with the short end of the stick."} At the moment we hear those words, we have a decision to make: do we chime in and add our own complaints about 'life' or do we REPEL those words and attitudes? We must not accept them into our heart or embrace them as a way of life. We don't have to be rude with our response. Nobody likes a "holier than thou" approach. Remember, "for all have sinned and fall short of the glory of God" (Romans 3:23). Even if our response includes a form of correction, it can be spoken with love. Offer them compassion for their pain or difficulty, then, offer hope in God's faithfulness to work things out. Many times, words of correction and encouragement are accepted, yet, there are people who are 'dead set' in their pessimistic attitudes. We cannot become weary in our well doing. We must continue to sow seeds of righteousness and truth. We must also be teachable and correctable. There are times when we suffer 'battle fatigue' and allow our emotions to control our attitudes and speech.

"Listen to counsel and accept discipline,
That you may be wise the rest of your days."
Proverbs 19:20

Be humble and teachable:

"Come, you children, listen to me;
I will teach you the fear of the LORD.
Who is the man who desires life,
And loves length of days that he may see good?
Keep your tongue from evil,
And your lips from speaking deceit.
Depart from evil, and do good;
Seek peace and pursue it."
Psalm 34:11–14

Most human beings would choose life over death and

would add, not subtract, days to their life. They would prefer good things happening in their life, not bad. So, learning the "fear of the LORD" just might be a prudent thing to do!

First consider the meaning of the phrase: "the fear of the LORD." If one truly recognizes God as all-powerful, this will be reflected in his attitude and daily life in the form of *reverence.* The LORD is recognized as the sole Exerciser of power over the unwise and all mankind, as the Creator of the world and Disposer of life and death. If we walk 'in the fear of the LORD,' we will maintain a pious posture in which we perform practical functions in life. Have you ever met someone that is so 'spiritual' with their 'heads in the clouds' that they are of no 'earthly good?' We must not be so. We must maintain our (vertical) relationship with the LORD, while we perform practical functions (horizontally) during our life on earth. That's what Jesus did.

As our spiritual posture conforms to the 'fear of the LORD,' we watch and protect our tongues from releasing hurtful words. Why, 'protect?' Our witness for the Lord must be protected. Our injurious words can mar our testimony for God.

Our injurious words can mar our testimony for God.

We guard our hearts from harboring a negative attitude towards God. Our speech can promote honesty and integrity or deceitfulness and falsehood. What we choose will direct the course of our life, the length of our days and the good we will experience. When we refuse to accept inferior standards and *choose* to assume an upright posture, we will 'do good.'

Daily, we will anticipate, even ask God for, opportunities to speak the peace of Jesus over someone's life. We will be zealous in our speaking blessings for the benefit of others. We will hear from the throne room of God how to declare His will and way for others.

Say this aloud:

"I will set my face like flint upon the Lord. I will focus my eyes upon the Author and Finisher of my faith. I will speak the Word of Life over myself and others. I choose, this day, to serve the Lord with gladness, with a renewed and right spirit within me.
In Jesus' Name, so be it."

With great confidence in Who God is and what He has equipped and called us to do, we are prepared to speak blessings over others. We must ask God's Spirit to help us recognize opportunities to bless. Once we encounter the need, then, we ask Him for the appropriate Word. He will not disappoint us. He will be there to answer us because it is *His* desire to bless as He operates through us.

Raising children provides many opportunities for blessing them. When our youngest son, David, was five, he was overpowered by a fear of death and destruction. This occurred as he witnessed Cal and me discussing a natural gas leak at my parents' home. We were careful with our explanations, trying not to instill fear, but, fear grabbed hold of David's mind and spirit. For nights, I prayed and blessed him with confidence in the Lord's protection.

"David, may the Lord protect you from all evil.
May He protect your soul: your mind, will and emotions.
May the Lord guard your going out and your coming in from this time forth and forever more.
In Jesus' Name, Amen."

I affirmed God's protection over him. This allowed David to witness my confidence in God. Remember the importance of protecting the witness of our mouths. Our children NEED to observe our confidence in the Lord, in day-to-day situations.

As I mentioned in an earlier chapter, there are times at church when someone asks me to pray with them. I do pray with them, *and* I bless them. I differentiate between the two as I assume different postures for them. I compare these spiritual postures with physical ones. To accomplish different tasks, such as: bending to weed a garden, stooping to retrieve a dropped object, standing to help someone, we adjust our physical posture and position. We make adjustments to accomplish something. Likewise, in the spiritual realm, we assume various postures to execute different spiritual tasks, i.e.: expressing reverence to God, exercising faith, extending compassion, offering petitions to God, taking authority over the enemy, delivering God's timely message, teaching and preaching the gospel of Jesus Christ. The shift occurs as God's Spirit directs. He directs according to the *task at hand.* God's plans will be accomplished, here on earth, as they are in heaven.

. . . we assume various postures to execute different spiritual tasks . . .

Consider this example: you converse with someone, i.e.: your child or an employee. At a later time, you assume an authoritative position and instruct them to do something. You are communicating, yet, with a different posture or relational position. Your spiritual posture with speaking blessings is one of *authority, dominion* and *power;* that which is given to you by the Lord to speak forth His Word, trusting Him to perform it (Jeremiah 1:12).

Clearly, speaking blessings over others requires an unwavering confidence in God. With God, all things are possible (Matthew 19:26). Is there anything too hard for the Lord? (Genesis 18:14) There is no limit to His goodness, mercy and grace. When we confess Jesus' victory in troubling situations and believe in our hearts that life and a future reigns over death and destruction, then we will be saved out of those situations. We convey our faith to others as we assume a posture of faith. Read Romans 10:8–10. Go ahead, I'll wait for you. Pause for a moment and consider: this passage does not only apply to our eternal salvation and destiny. It also refers to our daily lives, emphasizing the affirmations of faith that originate in our hearts and are expressed through our mouths. Now, read Romans 9:33; 10:11–12. Jesus does not disappoint. He can be trusted. We must convey our trust to others. We must help others call upon and apply Jesus' name over their lives and their particular circumstances. Read Romans 10:13–15. We are to be a bearer of *glad tidings of great joy* which shall be for all the people (Luke 2:10). We are to serve God as messengers just as the angels delivered His message to the lowliest shepherds. There are many people around us who are functioning in a 'lowly' state of faith. They need our message of hope, faith and love.

. . . speaking blessings over others requires an unwavering confidence in God.

So, let all blessings flow. These ideas should help your creativity. Holy Spirit will direct the rest.

1.   The next time a telemarketer calls your house, listen to their promotional speech, then ask them if *you* can ask a question. Inquire if they are a believer in the Lord Jesus; if He is their Savior. Then, follow the lead of the Spirit. If they are a believer, ask if you could bless their day, or work, or family. I have done this on the phone! One day, I was explaining my frustration with a company's lack of response, when the sales person began listing all the difficulties that her company had suffered. By the Spirit's

leading, I asked if I could bless her. She said, "Hold on a minute." When the sales lady returned to the phone, she explained that she had turned on the speaker so her entire sales force could listen to my blessing! Now that is God's kind of multiplication: not just one person, but many were blessed! The eyes of many were refocused on God.

If the telemarketer is not a believer, express God's love for them and the eternal life He offers them.

A possible blessing would be: *"May the Lord bless you with His presence, allowing you to see Him in all His glory. May His truth touch your heart and comfort your soul. In Jesus' Name, Amen."*

2.   Bless your children in their 'going out' and their 'coming in.' Before your children leave for school, speak a blessing over them. When they are doing their homework, or studying for a test, release a blessing over their efforts.

"May the Lord cause you to prosper
and excel in all that you do.
May His favor surround you as a shield.
May you take joy in what you are asked to do.
May what you do bring honor to the Lord.
In Jesus' Name, Amen."

"May God's Spirit instruct and direct your studying.
May He give you 'Holy Spirit highlights,'
showing you what to study.
May your memory be blessed and increased.
May you make quick application of the information you
study to the questions on your test.
May the peace of our Lord Jesus guard
your heart and your mind.
In Jesus' Name, Amen."

3.   When you leave a phone message, bless the listener. Picture this: you return home, after a hard day at work, turn on the voice mail and hear someone speaking a blessing over you. It's like a cup of cool, refreshing water to a dry, parched throat. God's Word brings life and restoration, encouragement and love.

> *"Hello, my friend. I won't be able to*
> *attend your party, but I would*
> *like to speak a blessing over your efforts.*
> *May the Lord reward your work and your wages be full*
> *from the Lord, the God of Israel, under whose wings*
> *you have sought refuge.*
> *May God give you wisdom and understanding in the*
> *administration of your work.*
> *May He cause your hands to prosper.*
> *May you never cease to bless and praise the Lord!*
> *In Jesus' Name, Amen."*

4.   Sometimes you have family members or beloved friends who don't live near you. Sometimes, these same people aren't receptive to your words of faith. What's a 'faith-filled' person to do? Follow Naomi's lead: she spoke a blessing over Boaz even though he wasn't present. She trusted that God desired to bless Boaz and she was acting in faith that He would. Faith pleases God.

> *"Her mother-in-law then said to her,*
> *'Where did you glean today*
> *and where did you work? May he who*
> *took notice of you be blessed.'"*
> *"And Naomi said to her daughter-*
> *in-law, 'May he be blessed*
> *of the LORD who has not withdrawn his kindness*

> *to the living and to the dead.'"*
> **Ruth 2: 19, 20**

Cal and I have acted upon this principle of releasing spoken blessings over people who cannot hear us. Sometimes, actual miles separate us, but, in other situations, the conditions of hearts and emotions have been the separating factor. You know what I am talking about. Even though you live 'under the same roof,' family members are often isolated from each other. God wants unity: a house divided falls. So, during our prayer time every morning, we have spoken blessings over loved ones.

> *"May you,_____, love the Lord with*
> *all your heart, soul, mind and strength.*
> *May you truly love your neighbor*
> *as yourself. May others see in you the love of Christ.*
> *May God stir within you all the gifts and callings*
> *He has planned and purposed for your life.*
> *May you seek Him and understand His ways.*
> *May you embrace His truth so it*
> *becomes your rule of conduct.*
> *May you walk in a manner worthy of His calling.*
> *May God give you wisdom beyond your years,*
> *surpassing your training and knowledge.*
> *May all that you do be done to honor Him.*
> *In Jesus' Name, Amen."*

> *"[insert person's name], may the Lord*
> *be your shield and your defense.*
> *May you be afraid of no one. May He bring you*
> *comfort through His Word, His Worship*
> *and through His Warfare.*
> *May you be strong in the Lord and*
> *in the power of His might.*

*May you tear down the strongholds that bind and
restrict your walking in His covenant promises.
May you know Him as your Victor.
In Jesus' Name, Amen."*

I am and you are God's ambassador proclaiming His
truth and eternal destiny for His people. With great
confidence, we can draw near to the throne of God,
asking for and receiving His mercy and grace for ourselves and for others (Hebrews 4:16). God will give
us the words to speak to make known with boldness
the truth of His Word. Truth dispels lies. Lies trap
and hinder people from becoming all that God purposed for them; aborting their eternal inheritance.

We didn't give up.

---

5. Just as Jesus is 'preparing a place for us' (John 14:2),
    prepare your heart and life for children yet to be 'born'
    into your family, whether through your natural body,
    foster care or through adoption. Begin speaking aloud
    the fruitfulness of your body, male or female. Cal and
    I spoke blessings over our bodies and our union many
    years before David was conceived. We didn't give up.
    We had to walk by faith and not by sight. Our physical
    bodies were aging, but we chose to believe the report of
    the Lord that children are His blessing (Psalm 127:3–5).
    God desires to give good gifts to us. Such tenacity is
    often needed, even in the lives of other couples desir-
    ing children. Cal and I have spoken blessings of fruit-
    fulness and multiplication over others. We have coupled
    this with continual prayer for them, calling forth children
    who will be raised for the glory of God and for the fur-
    therance of His Kingdom.

6.   Even if your children are young, begin to bless their future spouse. Call forth the preparation of your child and his/her spouse for a holy union; preserving their purity, righteousness and unity in the oneness of Christ. Cal and I began doing this many years ago. We continue to bless our children and their future spouses. Both Rebecca and Isaac brought individual blessings into their marriage which worked together to fulfill God's eternal destiny for them as a couple and for their descendants. Our oldest son, Anthony, has recently married Cassidy Webb of Sanford, Florida. Anthony began praying for his future spouse when he was around 10. Cal and I joined his prayers with blessings for him and his future bride. Now, our blessings are more specific, directed to the needs of this young couple.

7.   Exercise great faith in God as your provider as you speak blessings of success, prosperity and favor over your spouse. Identify their natural and supernatural abilities and encourage those areas with the power of God's Word. Under gird your spouse with blessings that build confidence in areas which challenge them. As Cal and I ride together to church on Sundays, I speak blessings over him as I massage his hands with cream. Rubbing his right hand, I speak:

"May the Lord strengthen you as you serve others.
May your hands be anointed for the
healing and comfort of others.
May the Lord reward your service.
May God prosper your work,
causing you to gain wealth.
May you honor God from your wealth.
May you always be a cheerful giver.

May the Lord give you wisdom and
counsel to do His work.
In Jesus' Name, Amen."

Then, I take his left hand, the one on which
he wears our wedding band, and speak:

"May our love for each other grow
more perfect and complete.
May we be united in our love for
the Lord and for each other.
May our love be sacrificial and full of joy.
May the Lord bless our marriage with His presence.
May He use our marriage to bless others.
In Jesus' Name, Amen."

8.   Allow your faith to be witnessed by other believers as you speak blessings over them. Every time you attend a church service, a class, a fellowship time or as you serve; ask God for and expect to encounter an opportunity to bless. There is always someone in your path who needs God's blessing. So, determine in your heart that you will be a blessing to the Body of Christ. You are God's ambassador. When you prepare your heart and focus your expectations, looking for blessing opportunities, your fellowship times will always be exciting and rewarding. "Church" will never be the same!

God's will is to bless.

---

9.   Remember: out of nothing can come something. God has shown us that from the beginning. We know and have experienced the power of His Word. And, His Word lives within us. Begin to speak blessings with confidence in Him.

If you live in a rural community, speak blessings of productivity and prosperity over the land. If the small towns in your area are "drying up," speak God's life over them. Speak blessings over your sphere of influence. Deuteronomy 28:3 proclaims: "Blessed shall you be in the city, and blessed shall you be in the country." God's will is to bless.

"May these fields be fruitful and multiply.
May the earth become rich with nutrients
and minerals. May the seed planted take
root and grow, producing a bountiful harvest.
May these crops be protected from destructive forces.
May the rains come at the proper time
and in the needed amounts.
May the Lord give the farmers wisdom and instruction
for the benefit of their investment.
May these farmers honor the Lord with their first fruits,
returning to Him a tenth of all their earnings.
May they praise and bless His Name.
In Jesus' Name, Amen."

"May the commerce of this town begin to flourish.
May life, not death, be restored to this area.
May a quickening occur within the minds and hearts
of these business people, showing them how to
operate in a profitable way.
May God's favor surround their businesses, drawing
others to use their services and to buy their products.
May these owners operate their stores and
lives in a manner worthy of the Lord. May
they honor Him in all their ways.
May the Lord cause their hands to prosper.
In Jesus' Name, Amen."

Your city, state and country will greatly benefit from your boldly proclaiming blessings over them. Read the Amplified Bible's version of Proverbs 11:11—

"By the blessing of the influence of
the upright and God's favor
[because of them] the city is exalted,
but it is overthrown by the mouth of the wicked."

Your influence upon your homeland carries weight and value. Become informed and sensitive to the needs of your city, state and country. Listen to the events which are occurring and address those specific needs within your blessings. With great faith, speak them over your land. God will honor your faith and will accomplish His plan.

"For the eyes of the LORD are in every place,
Watching the evil and the good."
Proverbs 15:3

"For the eyes of the LORD move to
and fro throughout the earth
that He may strongly support those
whose heart is completely His . . ."
II Chronicles 16:9

{*A Call to the Nation* blessing set was written for releasing blessings over our nation. Refer to Resources for ordering this set or create your own blessings for our nation.}

10.   If you need time to develop your confidence in *speaking* blessings, try this:

        a. Write a note, even a Thank You card, to someone and include a simple blessing.

"May the Lord bless you with His presence.
May He return to you the kindness
you have shown me.
May He honor your compassionate heart.
In Jesus' Name, Amen."

b. Send an e-mail to a college-aged child, to a friend or a business associate and include a blessing. In your blessing, address something that is important to them; i.e.: high test scores, financial support, success in their career, wisdom for parenting, etc. When you speak about something that is important to them and call upon God for His help, they will take notice.

c. If your spouse travels, write a blessing on a 3 x 5 card and slip in into their overnight bag. God's Word and your love will warm their heart.

"May God bless your going
out and your coming in.
May His favor surround you like a shield.
May others honor the character
of Christ they see in you.
May God give you wisdom in your business.
May His Spirit direct your thoughts.
May you respond to His leading.
May you always remember that God loves you
with an everlasting love that doesn't end.
In Jesus' Name, Amen."

d. If your spouse is not receptive for such an overt expression of your faith, go "undercover," literally. A friend placed blessings under her husband's side of their bed, between the mattress and box springs.

Once she began doing this, she testified to noticing a difference in his mental and spiritual attitudes. She coupled this effort with speaking blessings over him out of his hearing and continually prayed for him and his salvation. Remember, it is the power of God, present through His Word, which accomplishes His work of redemption, restoration, healing, deliverance, etc. This same power was at work through Peter's shadow (Acts 5:15) and Paul's handkerchiefs and aprons (Acts 19:11–12). It is not the piece of paper or cloth, but the anointing: the powerful presence of God that operates through something or someone to perform His will. His Word carries His anointing.

e. If your children are in the public school system, you can share God's blessings in several ways: (1.) for his teachers, prepare baked goods or candy bags and attach a blessing to each bag; (2.) during Teacher Appreciation Week, place a written blessing in every teacher's 'mailbox;' (3.) during Thanksgiving activities in which parents participate, share a written blessing and note of thanks for their faithful support. Keep in mind that every child is helped when parents give of their time and resources.

f. If your children attend a Christian-based school, your efforts could include the children. A friend has shared blessings with her son's classmates year after year. She has found creative ways to distribute blessings to these students who express anticipation for their special blessing. Some students have taken their blessing home and shared it with their parents! What precious treasures have been given by this one mother! You can do this as well.

g. At a gathering of friends (i.e.: a ladies' luncheon, or a dinner for couples), place a blessing at the place setting of each guest. Ask each guest to read aloud their blessing. As each blessing is read, the encouraging Word is multiplied beyond just the individual reading it. The atmosphere of your gathering is turned to honoring the Lord and expecting Him to work in the lives of your guests. As I have attended luncheons in which this was done, I have heard the guests testify that their blessing specifically addressed a need in their life. This has truly humbled me to witness the power of God and His loving-kindness.

h. During the early 1990's, I served as the children's pastor for Christian Heritage Church in Tallahassee, Florida. Desiring to develop a different approach to observing the Advent Season, the Lord gave me 'a witty invention:' the Blessing Wreath. The first one developed had 24 written blessings attached to it. Each blessing was rolled and tied with ribbon. Also, special treats wrapped in colorful fabric were tied to the evergreen wreath. The wreath was placed on a table with a pillar candle positioned within its center. Beginning December 1st, the candle was lit at dinnertime and a child would select a blessing which was read aloud over him and others. The children were allowed to take one treat after the blessing was spoken over them. Each night a different child was allowed to choose a blessing, but *all heard* the spoken Word for their life. The speaking of these blessings offered opportunities for family discussions about the meaning of the blessing and their expectations of God's doing great things in their lives.

Reading these prepared blessings allowed parents time to become familiar with the idea of speaking blessings. The pressure of performing was removed. Over time, the parents observed the excitement of their children wanting their blessing read. As the evenings progressed, parents felt more comfortable with speaking blessings. To complete the 31 days of December, parents were encouraged to create and write blessings which were personalized for their children and their specific needs and interests. Something so very simple has been powerful and significant in the lives of children. They desperately need encouragement and affirmations. They need to hear of God's love for them and witness the faith of their parents.

The anticipation of Jesus coming into our lives and doing great things in us and through us is comparable to an Advent study of the coming of our Messiah. We honor who Jesus is, God with us, as the blessings focus our attention to Him and His presence within our lives. Such a time of spiritual reflection can encourage "making room" for Jesus to live and operate within our hearts and homes.

My desire is for families to develop the practice of speaking blessings over each other. If you are interested in using the Advent Blessing

Wreath within your family, business, Sunday School class, church or school, contact:
blessingsetc@hellensuniforms.com
to order. 24 written blessings are included, along with 7 blank papers for your personalized inscription. Begin a new tradition which honors the Lord and encourages excitement for life and hope for the future!

Learn to bless God. One of the reasons for speaking blessings over people is to turn their attention to God and to focus on His character and nature. We must do the same. As we experience His power and presence within our lives and recognize His blessings flowing into our lives, praise will pour forth from our hearts. We will honor Him with our lips. We will exalt Him with our worship. Psalms 145–150 are beautiful examples of blessing our God. Consider the various attributes of God's character that are identified: great, glorious, majestic, powerful, good, gracious, merciful, everlasting, righteous, just, delivering, protective, supportive, healing, providing, creative, etc. Confess aloud these attributes and ascribe them to God. As we learn how to bless Him, we will be endued with His power. It never fails.

When I bless and thank Him for who He is, I declare His nature over my loved ones, myself and over every situation. Consequentially, I am empowered with confidence in His presence operating within my life.

Try this. Focus on Him. With a pure heart, honor Him with your words. Declare who He is over your life. In blessing God, you will be blessed.

11. Speak blessings filled with life, restoration and peace over those struggling with health problems: body, soul or spirit. Jesus came to give us life and life abundantly. You will encounter people with varying types and degrees of illnesses. Jesus is the Healer of all conditions and diseases. Even if the illness has caused a loss of mental acuteness, you can exercise faith and speak the Word of Life to the person's spirit. Jesus will honor your faith and respond to the declared Word just as He did to the centurion's faith which is documented in Matthew 8:5–13. Every person has an eternal spirit which does not 'shut down,' even if the mind does. Using the Word of God, speak spirit to spirit.

12. Catch the Lord's vision of your being His ambassador. As you go forth and release His spoken Word into people's lives, you are expressing and imparting the King's will into their lives. When you accept the ministry of reconciliation and begin to use the word of reconciliation, you become a vital link to the eternal restoration of thousands. Restoring people to their "right relationship" with the Father is the reason for Jesus' humbling Himself to become a human, suffering death on the cross and receiving new life. You honor and exalt Jesus' life, death and resurrection when you speak blessings over others.

My Blessing for You

"May you be kind and tender-hearted to others, forgiving them, just as God in Christ has forgiven you.

May you bless others, even when
they curse or mistreat you.
May God sow His life-changing
seed in your life.
May you become a tree firmly planted by
streams of water, which yields its fruit in its
season, and whose leaf does not wither.
May you sow the seeds of life and truth.
May you reap a great harvest of righteousness.
May God cause you to prosper
in whatever you do.
May whatever you do be done
to the glory of God.
In Jesus' Name, Amen

Journal of My Journey with the Spoken Blessing

Refer to Luke 7:11–17 in which Jesus redirected the widow's focus from her dead son to hope for the future. Examine your outlook on life. List areas that need a new approach. Explain what you will do to change your heart, your focus and your confession to one of *life, hope* and *confidence* in the Lord.

_____

_____

_____

_____

_____

_____

_____

_____.

How do you plan to keep your heart and your speech pure?

_____

_____

_____

_____

_____.

What scriptures have made the most impact on confirming to you the necessity, validity, and power of speaking blessings over yourself and others, over your community and nation?

_____

_____

_____

_____

_____

_____

_____

_____.

Write a blessing that will impart God's *favor, blessing* and *increase* into a person's life. Ask God for an opportunity to speak it over someone.

_____

_____

_____

_____

_____.

"Do nothing from selfishness or empty conceit, but with humility of mind let each of you regard one another as more important than himself; do not merely look out for your own personal interests, but also for the interests of others."
Philippians 2:3–4

Appendix

Examples of Blessings

1. HUSBANDS, FRIENDS, CO-WORKERS, CHILDREN:

"May the LORD reward your work, and your wages be full from the LORD, the God of Israel, under whose wings you have sought refuge." Ruth 2:12

"May God's favor surround you like a shield." Psalm 5:12

"May God cause you to prosper and excel in all that you do. May whatever you do bring honor and glory to God." Genesis 39:3; Colossians 3:17; I Peter 4:11

2. CHILDREN:

"May the Lord protect you from all evil. May He keep your soul. May the Lord guard your going out and your coming in from this time forth and forever more." Psalm 121:5–8

This blessing can be used with different ages. Young children may become fearful of the dark, storms or scary noises. Older children may have concerns about attending a large high school, gangs, drugs, etc. Young adult children may feel uncertain about leaving for college.

"May you remember that you can do all things through Christ who strengthens you." Philippians 4:13

A child or teenager may struggle with a poor self-image. Remind them of the power of Jesus working within them through His Spirit.

"May God hold you in His loving arms, embracing you with His compassion. May you feel the warmth of His presence and know that He will never leave you or forsake you. You are His and He is yours." Joshua 1:5

This blessing can be applied to various situations of children being apart from their parents, i.e.: spending the night with a friend, attending summer camp, children leaving for college or beginning a new job.

"May you know that God has loved you with an everlasting love, and that He draws you to Him with His loving-kindness." Jeremiah 31:3

You could encourage and bless a child or friend who struggles with recognizing God's love for them. Some children have been told that they were "accidents" or a "mistake." They need God's Truth spoken to them. Some marriage relationships undermine the worth of a person. Help a friend know the value God places on them.

3.   **FRIENDS:**
"May the Lord be your Good Shepherd caring and providing for all your needs. May He cause you to lie down in green pastures. May He lead you beside quiet waters. May He restore your soul." Psalm 23:1–3

Consider a friend who is experiencing difficult circumstances. Offer these encouraging words of God's Truth.

Creating Blessings from the Word

Use the following scriptures to develop blessings. Then, ask God for opportunities to speak them.

"The LORD is your keeper;
The LORD is your shade on your right hand.
The sun will not smite you by day,
Nor the moon by night.
The LORD will protect you from all evil;
He will keep your soul.
The LORD will guard your going out and your coming in
From this time forth and forever."
Psalm 121:5–8

May the Lord

_____
_____
_____
_____
_____
_____
_____
_____
_____
_____.

"'For I know the plans I have for you,' declares
the LORD, 'plans for welfare and not
for calamity to give you a future and a hope.'"
Jeremiah 29:11

"... and hope does not disappoint, because
the love of God has been poured out
within our hearts through the Holy Spirit who was given to us."
Romans 5:5

May you always remember

_____
_____
_____
_____
_____
_____
_____
_____
_____
_____.

"I will instruct you and teach you in
the way which you should go;
I will counsel you with My eye upon you."
Psalm 32:8

"But let all who take refuge in Thee be glad,
Let them ever sing for joy;
And mayest Thou shelter them,
That those who love Thy name may exult in Thee.
For is it Thou who dost bless the righteous man, O LORD,
Thou dost surround him with favor as with a shield."
Psalm 5:11,12

May God instruct

_____
_____
_____
_____

_____
_____
_____
_____
_____
_____.

*"that He would grant you, according to the riches of His glory,
to be strengthened with power through
His Spirit in the inner man;"*
Ephesians 3:16

*"For God has not given us a spirit of timidity, but of power
and love and discipline."*
II Timothy 1:7

May God strengthen you

_____
_____
_____
_____
_____
_____
_____
_____.

*"For I am confident of this very thing,
that He who began a good work
in you will perfect it until the day of Christ Jesus."*
Philippians 1:6

"Be diligent to present yourself approved to God as a workman
who does not need to be ashamed,
handling accurately the work of truth."
II Timothy 2:15

May you be confident

_____

_____

_____

_____

_____

_____

_____

_____

_____ .

"Children, obey your parents in the Lord, for this is right.
Honor your father and mother (which is the first commandment
with a promise), that it may be well with you,
and that you may live long on the earth."
Ephesians 6:1–3

May you obey

_____

_____

_____

_____

_____

_____

_____

_____ .

Journal of My Journey with the Spoken Blessing

After speaking blessings over others, describe to whom you spoke them and how they responded.

_____
_____
_____
_____
_____
_____
_____
_____
_____
_____
_____
_____.

Keep a log of the blessings you create from the Word and with whom you share them. Make observations of how the Lord responds to these blessings.

_____
_____
_____
_____
_____

_____

_____

_____

_____

_____

_____

_____.

Notate any unexpected responses to your spoken blessings. Describe your reactions to these responses.

_____

_____

_____

_____

_____

_____

_____

_____

_____

_____

_____.

"... while we have opportunity, let us do good to all men ..."
Galatians 6:10

References

A Life God Rewards
Multnomah Publishers, Inc., 2002

Bruce Wilkinson
with David Kopp

All the Women of the Bible
All the Divine Names & Titles in the Bible
Zondervan Publishing House, 1975

Dr. Herbert Lockyer, R.S.L.

Amplified Bible
Zondervan, 1987

Zondervan

Father Hunger
Servant Publications, 1993

Robert S. McGee

Give Me 40 Days
Bridge-Logos Publishers, 2002

Freeda Bowers

His Needs Her Needs
Fleming H. Revell, 2001

Willard F. Harley, Jr.

Imparting the Blessing to Your Children
Shalom, Inc., 1989

William T. Ligon, Sr.

Interpreting the Symbols and Types
Bible Temple Publishing, 1992

Kevin J. Conner

Seven Days of Stillness: A Prayer Focus
to Renew Your Spirit 08–31–04
Glory of Zion International Ministries

Chuck D. Pierce

Tallahassee Democrat, 08–02–99
Knight Ridder

Julie Sevrens

The Hebrew-Greek Key Study Bible
King James Version
Baker Book House, 1984

Spiros Zodhiates, Th. D.

The New Strong's Exhaustive   James Strong, LL.D., S.T.D.
Concordance of the Bible
Thomas Nelson Publishers, 1990

The Ryrie Study Bible   Charles C. Ryrie,
New American Standard Translation   Th. D., Ph.D.
Moody Press, 1978

The Works of Josephus   William Whiston, A.M.
Hendrickson Publishers, 1987

Vine's Expository Dictionary of Old and   W. E. Vine
New Testament Words
Marshall, Morgan & Scott, Publications,
Ltd., 1981

Webster's New World Dictionary of the   The World Publishing Co.
American Language
The World Publishing Company, 1968

Resources

Additional resources by Ann Dews Gleaton are listed below.
To order, contact her at:
E-Mail: blessingsetc@hellensuniforms.com

To request Ann as your guest speaker, call her at
1–850–222–1542
or to order more copies of *The Spoken Blessing*
contact Ann or, Tate Publishing, LLC.
1–405–376–4900

"Confidence—Who Needs It?" Ann presents a motivating message on the power of being confident in our approach to life. How we communicate our assurance about ourselves and our future will affect our overall outlook and how others perceive us. She explains, through biblical examples, our source of confidence. This teaching is available on CD or Audio cassette.

CD	$ 9.95
Audio	$ 5.95

Ann has written a series of blessing sets designed to help you begin speaking the blessings of God into your life. The following descriptions will assist you in selecting a special set that will transform you and those about you by the power of God's Word. These sets are written on parchment paper, then rolled and tied with ribbons. They are to be read aloud each day. Wreaths have been designed to support several of the blessing themes. Their prices will be noted. Other blessing sets have been incorporated within decorative containers whose prices range from $9.95 to $24.95. Blessing sets can be purchased separately for $6.00 unless otherwise noted.

A Call to the Nation Fellow Americans, this patriotic wreath is for you! The brass horn attached to the 18" grapevine wreath calls believers to pray and to bless our nation. Written as a large scroll, the 40 blessings carry a message of earnest intercession for our country. Speak the Living Word into the backbone of America. Call our nation back to its first love: Jesus. Order this wreath in preparation for celebrating our nation's independence and liberty!

18" Grapevine wreath $41.95

40 blessings individually rolled and tied $10.00

A Future and a Hope Think of the BEST gift you could give to that special graduate. Now, consider giving them God's Word through blessings which impart His wisdom, favor, blessing and increase. These blessings will encourage them to focus on God's love for them and His will for their life.

A Place of Refuge These blessings of solace and faith are attached to a unique table top wreath. It is the perfect gift of perpetual encouragement and healing. Consider a friend who is struggling with an illness and needs the Living Word spoken daily. This wreath can sit upright on a hospital tray or next to a bed. The petite roses never die, serving as a constant reminder of Jesus and His never dying love.

14" Grapevine Table Top wreath $35.95

Apples of Truth This cheerful, 18" grapevine wreath honors all who teach. The colorful ribbon "measures" the distance many have traveled and the lengths they have gone to offer wisdom, knowledge, creativity and love to their students. Give the gift that reminds that special teacher that she or he is the apple of God's eye (Psalm 17:8). Your gift can be personalized on the miniature chalkboard.

18" Grapevine wreath $34.95

Come Away My Beloved Marriage is a wonderful and holy covenant in the eyes of the Lord. As you give this gift, you share Words of Life with the newlyweds. When they read aloud the blessings to each other, their hearts will be united by the life-changing power of God's Word. The 18" grapevine wreath is ornamented with creamy blossoms and flowing ribbon.

18" Grapevine wreath $43.95

Comfort and Encouragement These blessings offer con-solation and reassurance that God is aware of our needs and is attentive to the cries of our hearts. A daily dose of these encour-aging blessings can help someone change their focus from their troubles to their Solution, whose name is Jesus.

Cornerstones of God's Word These blessings convey the simple truth of the Father's love and forgiveness, the Son's sac-rifice and the Spirit's comfort and instruction. Read them daily and they will impact your faith and life.

18" Decorated silk pine wreath $32.95
18" Advent Wreath—assembly required $19.95

Fishers of Men May an attitude of evangelism be mul-tiplied within your heart as you read and speak these blessings. Meditate on the call of Jesus to become fishers of men (Matthew 4:19; Mark 1:17). Consider the significance of this 18" wreath's decorations—the net, the 3-strand cord, the boat, the Bible and the pole with just one fish. This is a unique gift for that special fisherman or woman in your life.

18" Grapevine wreath $37.95

His Dwelling Place Each of us desires our home to reso-nate with the sounds of love, laughter and happy hearts. May your heart and home abound with the love of the Lord as you read aloud these blessings. May your focus be sharpened to see God's desires for your home. As your outlook is renewed, may you begin to speak with confidence these blessings over your family. May the atmosphere of your home reflect the glory of His presence. The wreath is designed with greenery, dainty flowers and a floral bow. This wreath makes a great "housewarming" gift.

18" Grapevine wreath $38.95

His Harvest See the "lost" through the eyes of God. Feel His compassion, yearn for the masses to know the Son. Hear the word of the Lord as you read aloud these blessings. Allow God's Holy Spirit to instruct you and direct your path every day. Discover the joy of telling others about your Lord Jesus.

These blessings can be attached to an 18" grapevine wreath which is decorated with varying shades of gold, red and rust florals.

18" Grapevine wreath $49.95

Holiness and Purity These blessings challenge every believer to walk in a manner worthy of their calling (Ephesians 4:1). Jesus identified the reward of possessing a pure heart . . . seeing God (Matthew 5:8). This set of blessings can be attached to a silk pine wreath decorated with snowmen and red berries.

18" Silk pine wreath $38.95

Hope: The Anchor of the Soul Everyone needs hope. Hope for a better tomorrow sustains many people during their tough times. Share these encouraging blessings with someone who needs uplifting. Help them focus on the One who is their Hope.

These blessings can be attached to the wreath of your choice or included in a decorative container.

Hope: The Anchor of the Soul Translated into Spanish, these blessings are for your friends who do not speak English. Minister to the nations with the Word.

Intimacy with the Lord Draw near to God and He will draw near to you (James 4:8). Call upon God and He will be there for you (Psalm 145:18). Proverbs 3:32b confirms that the Lord is intimate with the upright. These blessings speak to you about your special time with the Lord. He desires to have that quiet time with you. These blessings are often tucked inside a beautiful cup and saucer, as if to say: "take time for tea. . . . take time for the Lord."

Cup and saucer with blessings $24.95

Reflections of His Love This is a precious Baby Shower or New Baby gift, unlike any others. Both mother and baby will receive heartfelt blessings—God's life imparted into them as these blessings are spoken. Our lacy 18" wreath is accented with pastel plaid ribbon which coordinates with alphabet blocks. Baby's first booties hold the treasured blessings. These blessings can be used during a Baby Shower for a time of prayer and ministry. Multiples of this set have been given to local pregnancy support centers which offer them to their clients.

18" Lacy wreath $36.95
Blessing set prepared for Baby Shower $ 9.95

The Bread of Life Just imagine walking into a kitchen filled with the warmth and aroma of all your favorite foods, knowing someone has lovingly prepared them for you. You can offer your family such an inviting atmosphere as your heart is stirred with the reading and hearing of these "kitchen" blessings. As you experience Jesus' love for you, your cup will be filled to overflowing. May you serve the Bread of Life to your family and friends.

18" Grapevine wreath $44.95
Measuring cup with blessings $ 9.95

The Glow of His Light From Genesis to Revelation,

LIGHT represents the presence of God. We have been called out of darkness into His marvelous light (I Peter 2:9). Jesus called us to be "the light of the world" (Matthew 5:14). In John 8:12, Jesus declares Himself to be "the light of the world." Share His message of light with others. These blessings can be added to any wreath or tucked inside a special gift basket.

Blessing set $10.00

The Secrets of the Heart The Lord knows the secrets of our hearts (Psalm 44:21; 139:1,2). These blessings direct one's attention to friendship: with the Lord and with others. They will know we are Christians by our love (John 13:35). Touch the heart of another with this special gift. These blessings can be added to any wreath.

The Secrets of the Heart Translated into Spanish, these blessings about friendship can be shared with your Spanish-speaking friends. They will be delighted to have the Word written in their native language.

The Seed of God's Word Allowing God to prepare, plant and cultivate the seed of His word into your life is the focal point of these blessings. The 18" grapevine wreath boasts a variety of miniature vegetables which are graced with a sunflower ribbon. Careful introspection is encouraged as you read and speak these blessings every day. May you hear the Word of the Lord allowing it to grow, bearing fruit in your life.

18" Grapevine wreath $36.95

Walking in His Grace One of the most complex jobs with the least amount of formal education is that of parenting. Parents need to be reminded of God's steadfast love for them and for their children. The focus of these blessings is to encourage parents to not grow weary of well-doing, to remember the high calling of God upon their lives and to renew within them the commitment to see Jesus' victory in all circumstances. These blessings can be added to any wreath or container.

Walking in the Covenant When God created Adam and Eve, He desired to share an intimate, loving relationship with them. His desire to share a covenant relationship with each of us continues. Read these blessings to be reminded of the precious friendship that is waiting for you through the Lord Jesus. This 18" grapevine wreath is decorated with magnolia blossoms, greenery and berries.

18" Grapevine wreath $52.50

With a Life of Worship Our highest calling in life is to worship God. These blessings exhort every believer to honor their Lord with their love, their life and their laudation. Read a blessing every day. Keep your focus on your high calling.

This set can be attached to any wreath design, gift basket or special container.

With Fullness of Heart—A Mother's Blessing There are 31 blessings in this set—one for each day of the month. Daily, speak a blessing over your children. Near or far away, your children need your words of confidence in God for their lives.

Whenever God's Word is spoken in faith, He will respond (Jeremiah 1:12). If a child is leaving home, give him/her a set to read each day and reassure them that you are speaking a similar blessing over them. Remember this set for honoring someone on Mother's Day.

Blessing set $10.00

You Are Loved Many do not realize the true depth of God's love for us. These blessings will fill you with the love of Jesus which "bears all thing, believes all things, hopes all things, and endures all things" (I Corinthians 13:7). Allow these blessings to impart the deep love of God for you and your loved ones so that you will have confidence that God's love never fails (I Corinthians 13:8). Using this set, we can create a beautiful wreath or gift to celebrate someone's birthday, Valentine's Day, Mother's or Father's Day or Grandparent's Day.

Contact author Ann Dews Gleaton
or order more copies of this book at

TATE PUBLISHING, LLC

127 East Trade Center Terrace
Mustang, Oklahoma 73064

(888) 361 - 9473

Tate Publishing, LLC

www.tatepublishing.com